HABITAT Meerkats live in the desert areas of the southern part of Africa.

Atlantic Ocean

Pacific Ocean

Pacific Ocean

Indian Ocean

YOUNG Meerkats are adults when they are about one year old.

Habitat Each meerkat has a job to do in its community.

Senses Meerkats rely on their sense of smell to identify one another and to find food.

Science

Meerkat

Harcourt
SCHOOL PUBLISHERS

Orlando   Austin   New York   San Diego   Toronto   London

Visit *The Learning Site!*
www.harcourtschool.com

Printed in the United States of America

ISBN 0-15-345232-3

5 6 7 8 9 10   048   10 09 08 07

Meerkat

Consulting Authors

Michael J. Bell
Assistant Professor of Early Childhood Education
College of Education
West Chester University of Pennsylvania

Michael A. DiSpezio
Curriculum Architect
JASON Academy
Cape Cod, Massachusetts

Marjorie Frank
Former Adjunct, Science Education
Hunter College
New York, New York

Gerald H. Krockover
Professor of Earth and Atmospheric Science Education
Purdue University
West Lafayette, Indiana

Joyce C. McLeod
Adjunct Professor
Rollins College
Winter Park, Florida

Barbara ten Brink
Science Specialist
Austin Independent School District
Austin, Texas

Carol J. Valenta
Senior Vice President
St. Louis Science Center
St. Louis, Missouri

Barry A. Van Deman
President and CEO
Museum of Life and Science
Durham, North Carolina

Ohio Reviewers and Consultants

Linda Bierkortte
Teacher
Parkmoor Urban Academy
Columbus, Ohio

Napoleon Adebola Bryant, Jr.
Professor Emeritus of Education
Xavier University
Cincinnati, Ohio

Laurie Enia Godfrey
Director of Curriculum Development
Lorain City Schools
Lorain, Ohio

Christine Hamilton
Curriculum Specialist
Toledo Public Schools
Toledo, Ohio

Jerome Mescher
Science/Math Coordinator
Hilliard City Schools
Hilliard, Ohio

Cheryl Pilatowski
Science Support Teacher/Coordinator
Toledo Public Schools
Toledo, Ohio

Lisa Seiberling
Elementary Science Coordinator
Columbus Public Schools
Columbus, Ohio

Kathy Sparrow
Science Learning Specialist, K–12
Akron Public Schools
Akron, Ohio

Matthew Alan Teare
Science Resource Teacher
Miles Park Elementary School
Cleveland Municipal School District
Cleveland, Ohio

Shirley Welshans
Teacher
Parkmoor Urban Academy
Columbus, Ohio

EARTH AND SPACE SCIENCES

UNIT A:

Science Spin
Weekly Reader

Technology
An Assistant in Space, **56**

People
A First into Space, **58**

Science Spin
Weekly Reader

Technology
The Coldest Place on Earth, **88**

People
What's the Weather?, **90**

LIFE SCIENCES

UNIT B:

PHYSICAL SCIENCES

UNIT C:

OHIO EXPEDITIONS

Your Guide to Science in Ohio

Ready, Set, Science!

Vocabulary
inquiry skills
science tools
investigate

I wonder...

How can kids be scientists?

What do you wonder?

1

1

What Inquiry Skills Will We Use?

Fast Fact

A penny is like a sandwich made of metal. The inside layer is made of a metal called zinc. The outside layers are made of a metal called copper. You can observe coins to learn about them.

How Many Pennies?

You need

● pennies

● plastic jar

Step 1

Observe some pennies and a jar. Predict and write the number of pennies that will fill the jar.

Step 2

Fill the jar with pennies. Count the pennies that fit. Write the number.

Step 3

Compare the number of pennies in the jar with the number you predicted.

Inquiry Skill

When you observe, you can use your senses of sight and touch.

Reading in Science

SI-6 Use observations; **SI-7** Use scientific equipment and tools; **SI-8** Measure properties; **SI-10** Communicate explanations

VOCABULARY

inquiry skills

(Focus Skill) **READING FOCUS SKILL**

MAIN IDEA AND DETAILS Look for details about the inquiry skills that scientists use.

Inquiry Skills

Scientists use inquiry skills when they do tests. **Inquiry skills** help people find out information.

Observe

Use your five senses to learn.

Compare

Observe ways things are alike and ways they are different.

Classify

Classify things by sorting them into groups to show ways they are alike.

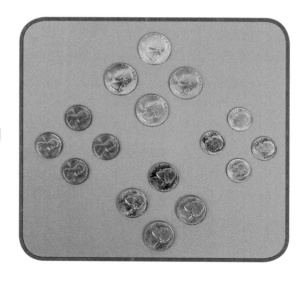

◀ sequence of size

◀ sequence of value

Sequence

Put things in order to show changes.

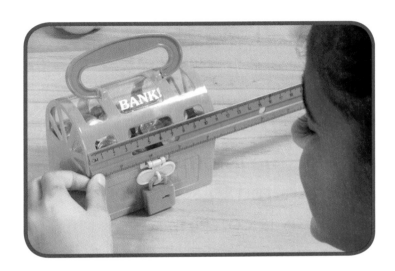

Measure

Use tools to find out how much.

Make a Model

Make a model to show what something is like or how it works.

Focus Skill MAIN IDEA AND DETAILS

What are some inquiry skills?

5

Hypothesize

Think of a scientific explanation that you can test.

A magnet attracts things made of iron.

The ball goes farther when I throw it hard. My hypothesis was right!

Draw Conclusions

Use all the information you have gathered to see if your hypothesis is correct.

Infer

Use what you know to make a good guess about what is happening.

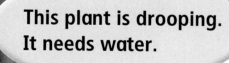

This plant is drooping. It needs water.

I think it's going to rain.

Predict

Use what you know to make a good guess about what will happen.

★ Focus Skill **MAIN IDEA AND DETAILS**
Why are drawing conclusions and predicting inquiry skills?

Stacking Pennies

Set a tray on a table. Predict what will happen if you try to stack 50 pennies. Stack the pennies on the tray. What happens? Was your prediction correct?

Plan an Investigation

Decide what you will do to find out what you want to know.

Communicate

Share what you know by showing or telling others.

MAIN IDEA AND DETAILS Why is communicating an inquiry skill?

1. MAIN IDEA AND DETAILS Copy and complete this chart. Tell details about the main idea.

Main Idea and Details

Inquiry skills help people find out information.

You **A** ____ two things when you observe ways they are alike and ways they are different.

You **B** ____ things when you put them in order.

You **C** ____ when you use what you know to make a good guess about what will happen.

2. SUMMARIZE Write two sentences that tell what the lesson is about.

3. VOCABULARY Use the term **inquiry skills** to tell about this picture.

Test Prep

4. What should you do if you want to find out how wide a box is?

Links

Writing

Sentences to Compare
Observe a penny and a nickel. Write a few sentences. Tell ways the penny and the nickel are alike and ways they are different.

 For more links and activities, go to www.hspscience.com

2

What Science Tools Will We Use?

Fast Fact

If you want to measure an object and you do not have a ruler or a tape measure, you can use your hand to see how many hands long the object is. You can predict a measurement and then measure to see if the prediction is correct.

Drops of Water on a Penny

You need

● dropper   ● cup of water   ● coin

Step 1

Predict the number of water drops you can put on a coin before the water runs off. Write your prediction.

Step 2

Use the dropper to drop water on the coin. Observe and count the drops. Stop when the water starts to run off the coin.

Step 3

Compare your prediction with the number of drops you were able to put on the coin.

Inquiry Skill
When you predict, you tell what you think will happen.

Reading in Science

SI-6 Use observations; **SI-7** Use scientific equipment and tools; **SI-8** Measure properties; **SI-9** Use numbers; **SI-10** Communicate explanations

VOCABULARY
science tools

 READING FOCUS SKILL

MAIN IDEA AND DETAILS Look for details about science tools.

Science Tools

When scientists want to find out about things, they use different tools. People can use these **science tools** to find out information.

Hand Lens

Use a hand lens to make objects look larger. Hold the hand lens near your face. Move the object until you see it clearly.

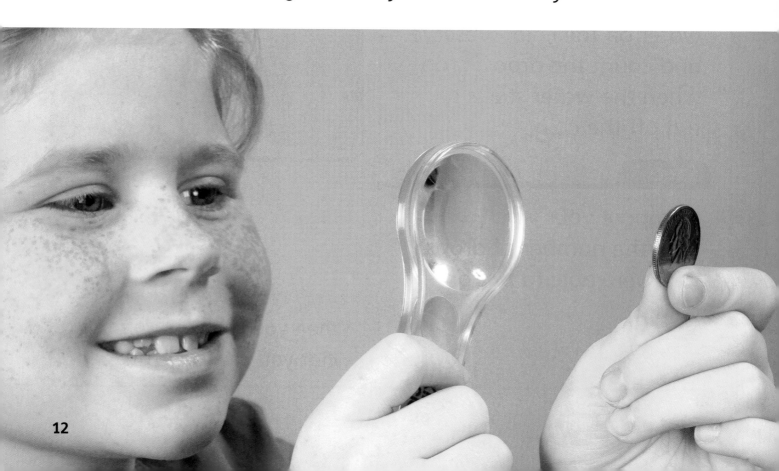

Magnifying Box

Use a magnifying box to make objects look larger. Place the object in the box, and look through the box.

Forceps

Use forceps to hold small objects or to separate them.

 **MAIN IDEA AND DETAILS** What are some objects you might want to use a hand lens to observe?

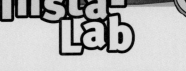

Observe a Coin

Use a hand lens to look at a coin. Then use a magnifying box to look at it. Draw what you observe.

Ruler

Use a ruler to measure length, width, and height. Put the first mark of the ruler at one end of the object. Read the number at the other end of the object.

Tape Measure

Use a tape measure to measure length, width, and height. Use a tape measure to measure around an object.

Dropper

Use a dropper to measure and place small amounts of liquid. Squeeze the bulb of the dropper. Put the dropper in the liquid and stop squeezing. To place drops of the liquid, slowly squeeze the bulb again.

Measuring Cup

Use a measuring cup to measure a liquid. Pour the liquid into the cup. Place the cup on a table. When the liquid stops moving, read the mark on the cup.

MAIN IDEA AND DETAILS

(Focus Skill) **Why is a measuring cup a useful science tool?**

Balance

Use a balance to measure the mass of an object. Place the object on one side of the balance. Place masses on the other side. Add or remove masses until the two sides of the balance are even.

Thermometer

Use a thermometer to measure temperature. Place the thermometer where you want to measure the temperature. Wait a few minutes. On the thermometer, read the number next to the top of the liquid.

MAIN IDEA AND DETAILS Why is a thermometer a science tool?

1. MAIN IDEA AND DETAILS Copy and complete this chart. Tell details about the main idea.

Main Idea and Details

Scientists use science tools.

A **A** ____ and a **B** ____ help you see small objects.	A **C** ____ holds small objects.	A **D** ____ and a **E** ____ measure length.	A **F** ____ and a **G** ____ measure liquids.	A **H** ____ measures temperature.

2. DRAW CONCLUSIONS How are a ruler and a tape measure alike? How are they different?

3. VOCABULARY Use the term **science tools** to tell about the lesson.

Test Prep

4. Which one would you use to look at something very small?
- **A.** a hand lens
- **B.** a measuring cup
- **C.** a ruler
- **D.** a thermometer

Links

Math

Estimate and Count

Estimate the number of pennies you need to make a row as long as a ruler. Then lay the pennies beside the ruler. Count the pennies. How many pennies did you need? Was the number of pennies more than, less than, or the same as your estimate?

 For more links and activities, go to www.hspscience.com

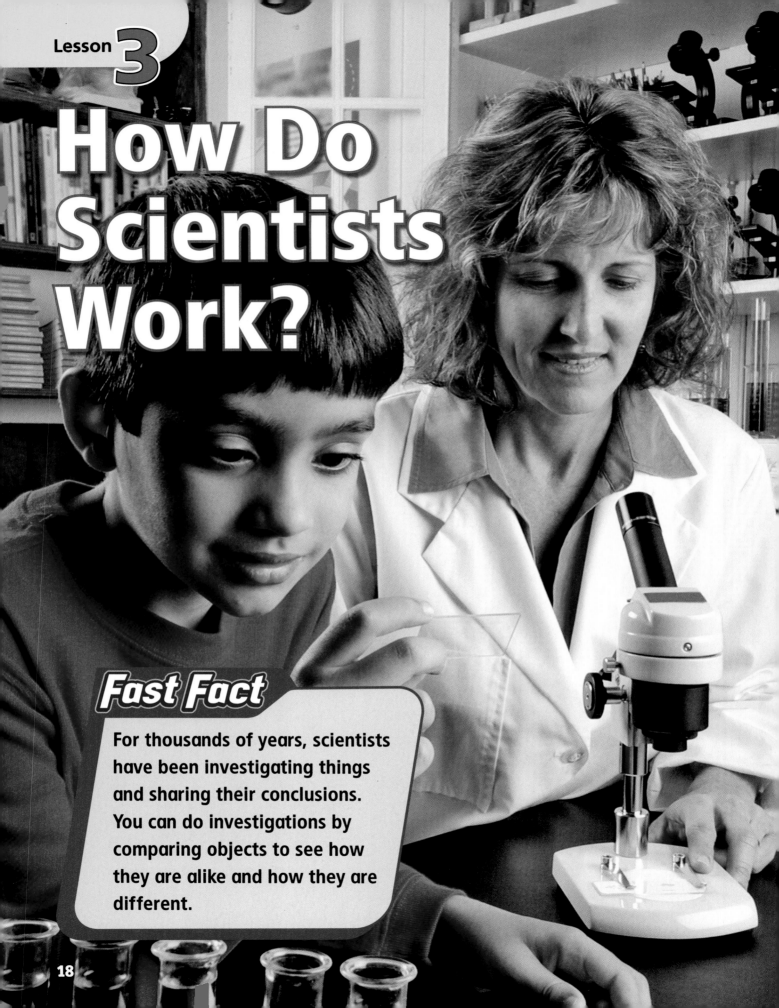

How Do Scientists Work?

Fast Fact

For thousands of years, scientists have been investigating things and sharing their conclusions. You can do investigations by comparing objects to see how they are alike and how they are different.

Equal Coins

You need

- quarter • 5 nickels • balance

Step 1

A quarter and 5 nickels both equal 25 cents. Does a quarter have the same mass as 5 nickels? **Compare** to find out.

Step 2

Make sure the balance is even. Then place the quarter on one side of the balance and the 5 nickels on the other side. Observe.

Step 3

Compare the two sides of the balance. Are they even?

Inquiry Skill

When you **compare**, you observe ways things are alike and ways they are different.

SI-6 Use observations; **SI-7** Use scientific equipment and tools;
SI-8 Measure properties; **SI-9** Use numbers

19

READING FOCUS SKILL

SEQUENCE Look for the order of the steps scientists use when they are investigating.

Investigating

When scientists want to answer a question or solve a problem, they **investigate**, or plan and do a test. When you investigate, you use a plan like this.

1. Observe, and ask a question.

Think of a question you want to answer. Write what you already know about the topic of your question. Figure out what information you need.

2. Form a hypothesis.

Write a hypothesis, or a scientific explanation that you can test.

Does the mass of a real quarter equal the mass of a play quarter?

The mass of a real quarter is greater than the mass of a play quarter.

3. Plan a fair test.

A fair test will help you answer your question. List things you will need and steps you will follow to do the test. Decide what you want to learn from the test.

4. Do the test.

Follow the steps of your plan. Observe carefully. Record everything that happens.

⭐ (Focus Skill) **SEQUENCE** What should you do after you form a hypothesis?

Insta-Lab

Wet Quarters

Wet a quarter. Place it on the mouth of a glass bottle. Wrap your hands around the bottle. What do you observe?

5. Draw conclusions, and communicate results.

Think about what you found out. Was your hypothesis correct? Use what you found out to draw conclusions. Then communicate your results with others.

Investigate more.

If your hypothesis was correct, ask another question about your topic to test. If your hypothesis was not correct, form another hypothesis and change the test.

My hypothesis was correct!

SEQUENCE What should you do before you draw conclusions?

Will a real dime have the same mass as a play dime?

1. SEQUENCE Copy and complete this chart. Tell about the way to investigate.

How to Investigate

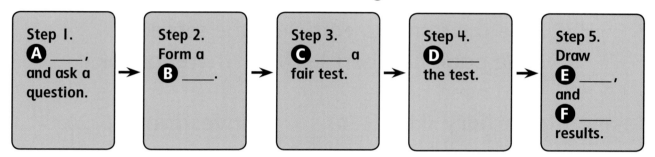

Step 1.
A ____, and ask a question.

→

Step 2.
Form a **B** ___.

→

Step 3.
C ___ a fair test.

→

Step 4.
D ___ the test.

→

Step 5.
Draw **E** ___, and **F** ___ results.

2. SUMMARIZE Write two sentences that tell what the lesson is about.

3. VOCABULARY Use the term **investigate** to tell about this lesson.

Test Prep
4. What is a hypothesis?

Links

Art

Coin Rubbings

Place coins under a sheet of paper. Use crayons of different colors to make rubbings of the coins. Label each coin with its name. Why can you make rubbings of coins?

 For more links and activities, go to **www.hspscience.com**

Review and Test Preparation

Vocabulary Review

Use the terms to complete the sentences. The page numbers tell you where to look if you need help.

inquiry skills p. 4   **investigate** p. 20
science tools p. 12

1. Comparing and measuring are two _____.

2. If you want to find out something, you can _____.

3. Scientists use _____ to find out information.

Check Understanding

4. Which of the following details is (Focus Skill) correct?

    A. A hand lens is an inquiry skill.
    B. Classifying is an inquiry skill.
    C. A dropper is an inquiry skill.
    D. A coin is an inquiry skill.

5. What is the next step you should do after you ask a question?

F. Investigate more.

G. Draw conclusions.

H. Plan a fair test.

J. Form a hypothesis.

Critical Thinking

6. Look at the picture.

Why are these things science tools?

7. Why must Miguel do a fair test if he wants to find out information?

UNIT A

Columbus

Wayne National Forest

Earth and Space Sciences

The chapters and features in this unit address these Grade Level Indicators from the Ohio Academic Content Standards for Science.

Chapter 1 The Solar System

ES-1	Recognize that there are more stars in the sky than anyone can easily count.
ES-2	Observe and describe how the sun, moon and stars all appear to move slowly across the sky.
ES-3	Observe and describe how the moon appears a little different every day but looks nearly the same again about every four weeks.

Chapter 2 Weather

| ES-4 | Observe and describe that some weather changes occur throughout the day and some changes occur in a repeating seasonal pattern. |
| ES-5 | Describe weather by measurable quantities such as temperature and precipitation. |

Unit A Ohio Expeditions

The investigations and experiences in this unit also address many of the Grade Level Indicators for standards in Science and Technology, Scientific Inquiry, and Scientific Ways of Knowing.

TO: diego@hspscience.com
FROM: shawna@hspscience.com
RE: Wayne National Forest

Dear Diego,

I'm in Wayne National Forest. You wouldn't believe how high the hills are! I was here last year in winter. The differences between the seasons are amazing!

Gotta climb,

Shawna

Experiment!

Evaporation As you do this unit, you will find out about weather and the water cycle. Plan and do a test. Make two puddles. See which one dries up first.

The Solar System

Vocabulary

solar system	moon
planet	season
orbit	
star	
constellation	
rotate	

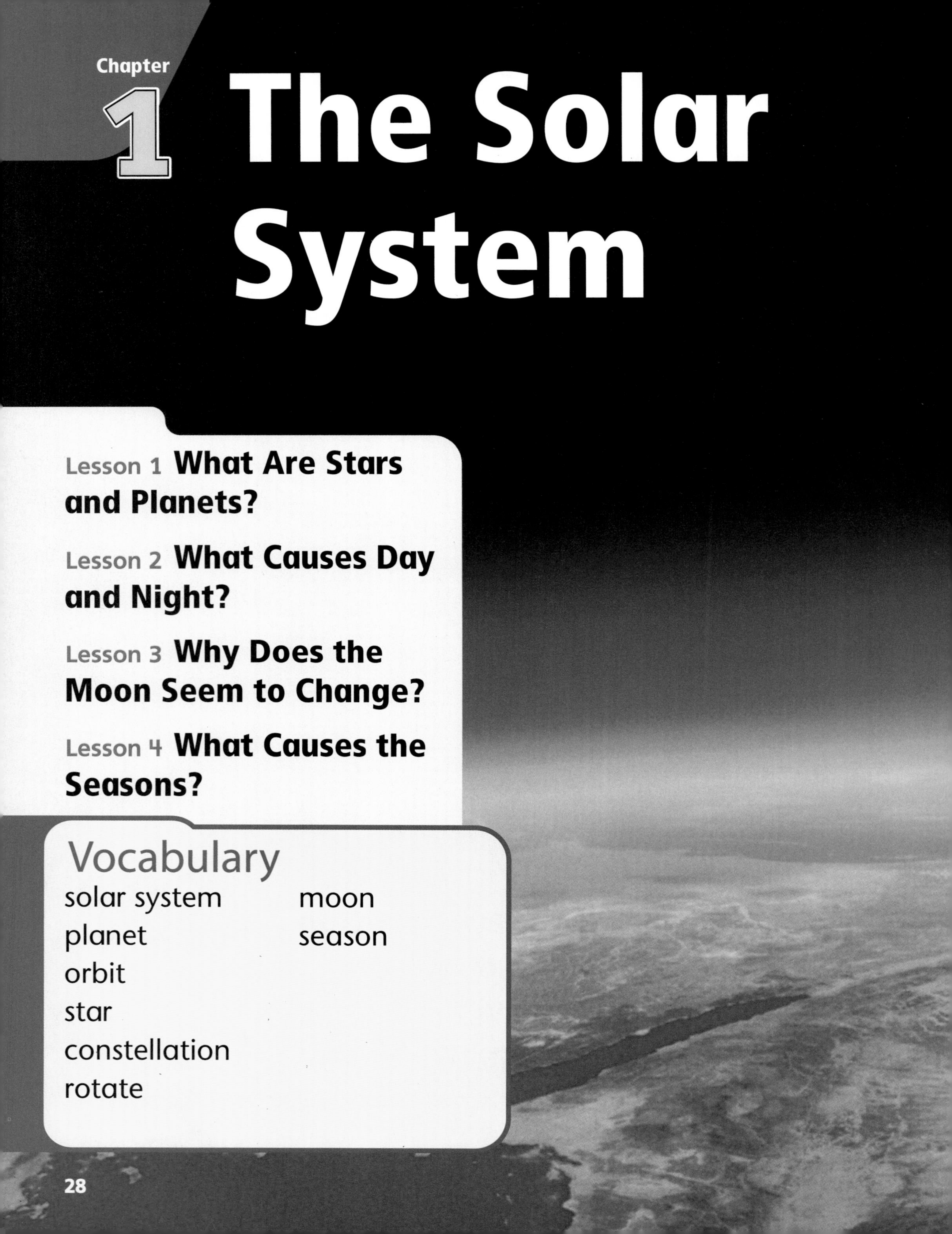

I wonder...

Why does the moon seem to move across the sky?

What do **you** wonder?

What Are Stars and Planets?

Fast Fact

There are too many stars to count easily. Most stars are seen only at night. You can infer why this is true.

Stars and Light

You need

- black paper

- tape

- "star" cup
- flashlight

Step 1

Tape the paper to a wall. Point the bottom of the cup toward the paper. Shine the flashlight into the cup. What do you observe?

Step 2

Turn off the lights. Shine the flashlight again. What do you observe now?

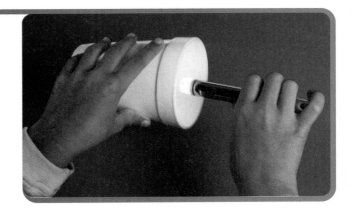

Step 3

Infer why the "stars" look different with the lights on and with the lights off.

Inquiry Skill

When you infer, you use what you see to figure out why something happened.

VOCABULARY

solar system
planet
orbit
star
constellation

READING FOCUS SKILL

MAIN IDEA AND DETAILS Look for details about the solar system.

The Solar System

The **solar system** is made up mainly of the sun, the planets, and the planets' moons. A **planet** is a large ball of rock or gas that moves around the sun. Earth is a planet in the solar system.

You can see the sun in the daytime. You can see a few other parts of the solar system at night. In the daytime, they are still there. You just can not see them when it is light outside.

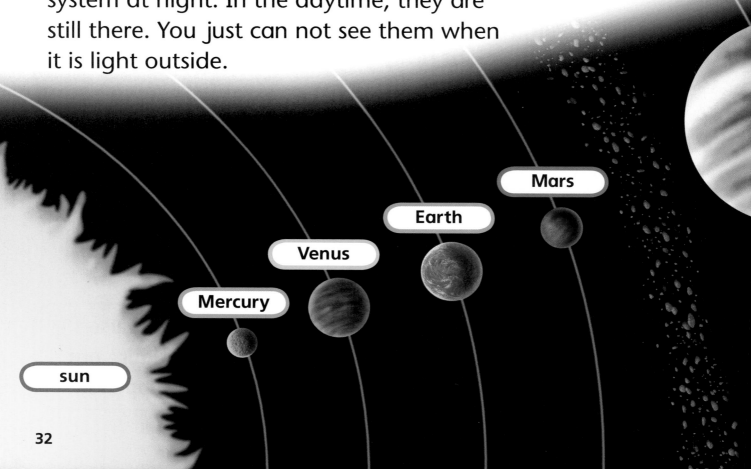

Mars

Earth

Venus

Mercury

sun

The sun is the center of the solar system. The nine planets move in paths around the sun. Each path is called an **orbit**.

The planets are different from one another. They look different. They are different sizes. They are at different distances from the sun, and they move in different orbits around it.

★ MAIN IDEA AND DETAILS
(Focus Skill) **What are the parts of the solar system?**

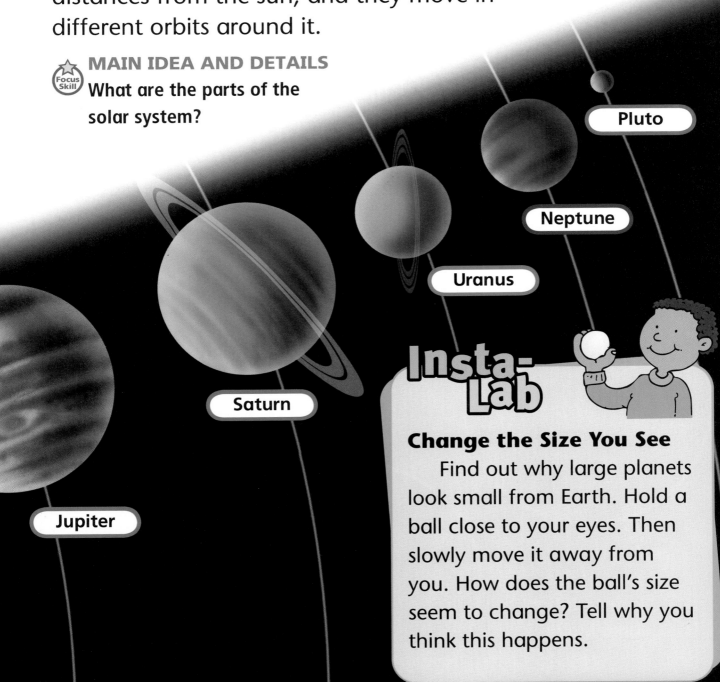

Pluto

Neptune

Uranus

Saturn

Jupiter

Insta-Lab

Change the Size You See
Find out why large planets look small from Earth. Hold a ball close to your eyes. Then slowly move it away from you. How does the ball's size seem to change? Tell why you think this happens.

Stars

A **star** is a huge ball of hot gases. The hot gases give off light and heat energy. The star closest to Earth is the sun.

You can see the sun in the daytime, but most stars can be seen only at night. There are more stars than anyone can easily count. Some stars are smaller than the sun. Others are bigger. They all look like tiny points of light because they are so far away. A group of stars that forms a pattern is called a **constellation**.

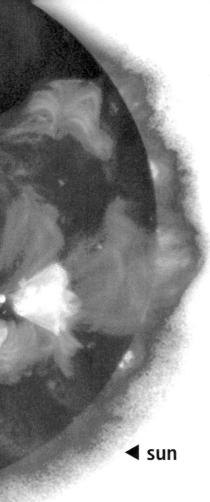

◄ sun

(Focus Skill) **MAIN IDEA AND DETAILS** What is a star?

▲ Orion

▲ Big Dipper, part of the constellation Ursa Major

◄ Little Dipper, part of the constellation Ursa Minor

1. MAIN IDEA AND DETAILS Copy and complete this chart. Tell details about the solar system.

Main Idea and Details

> The solar system is made up of the sun, the planets, and their moons.

> Earth is a **A** _____ in the solar system.

> The **B** _____ is the center of the solar system.

> The planets move in **C** _____ around the sun.

2. SUMMARIZE Write a lesson summary that uses the vocabulary terms.

3. VOCABULARY Use the terms **constellation** and **star** to tell about this picture.

Test Prep

4. Why can you NOT count stars easily?
  A. They look like points of light.
  B. You can not see them at night.
  C. Some are brighter than others.
  D. There are too many of them.

Links

Writing

Report About a Planet
Choose a planet. Find out four facts about it, and write a short report. Share your report with the class.

Mars
Mars is the fourth planet from the sun.
It is very dry on Mars.
Mars looks red from Earth.
It has two moons.

 For more links and activities, go to www.hspscience.com

2

What Causes Day and Night?

Fast Fact

Most parts of Earth have light and darkness each day because Earth is always spinning. You can observe the effects of Earth's movements.

Why Shadows Change

You need

- **two pieces of chalk of different colors**

Step 1

Stand outside in the morning. Have a partner trace your feet with chalk.

Step 2

Have your partner use chalk of a different color to trace your shadow.

Step 3

Wait two hours. Stand in the same place again. Have your partner trace your shadow again. Repeat two hours later. Communicate what you **observe**.

Inquiry Skill

When you **observe**, you use your senses to learn about things.

ES-2 Describe motion of sun, moon, stars; **SI-6** Use observations;
SI-10 Communicate explanations

VOCABULARY

rotate

READING FOCUS SKILL

CAUSE AND EFFECT Look for the effects of Earth's rotation on day and night and on shadows.

Earth's Rotation

It looks as if the sun rises in one place in the morning and sets in another place at night. The moon and the stars seem to move across the night sky. The sun, moon, and stars do not really move across the sky. It is Earth that is moving.

Earth spins around and around like a top. It takes about 24 hours for Earth to **rotate**, or spin, all the way around. One rotation, or spin, of Earth takes one day.

day

Earth's rotation causes day and night. Sunlight shines on only the part of Earth that is facing the sun. This side of Earth has daytime. The other side is dark. It has nighttime.

As Earth rotates, the part that was light turns away from the sun and gets dark. The part that was dark moves into the light. In most places, this pattern of day and night repeats every 24 hours.

★ **CAUSE AND EFFECT** **How does**
(Focus Skill) **Earth's rotation cause day and night?**

Insta-Lab

Model Day and Night

Put two pieces of tape on a globe in an X shape. Slowly spin the globe as you shine a flashlight on it. When is the tape in the light? When is it in the dark?

night

Changes in Shadows

When an object does not allow the sun's light to pass through it, it makes a shadow. Because Earth rotates, the sun seems to move. The sun's light shines on objects from different directions as the day goes on. This causes the sizes and shapes of shadows to change.

Look at the pictures to see how a shadow changes. When is the shadow long? When is it short? How does the direction the sun shines from change the shadow?

CAUSE AND EFFECT What causes shadows to change?

noon

morning

evening

1. CAUSE AND EFFECT Copy and complete this chart. Tell the effect of each cause.

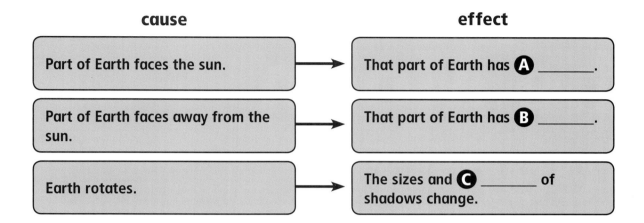

cause

| Part of Earth faces the sun. |
| Part of Earth faces away from the sun. |
| Earth rotates. |

effect

| That part of Earth has **A** _____. |
| That part of Earth has **B** _____. |
| The sizes and **C** _____ of shadows change. |

2. DRAW CONCLUSIONS How can you tell when the part of Earth where you live is facing away from the sun?

3. VOCABULARY Use the term **rotate** to tell why shadows change.

Test Prep

4. How does Earth's rotation make the sun seem to move?

Links

Math

Make a Bar Graph
Different planets have different numbers of hours in their days because they rotate at different speeds. Do research. Make a bar graph that shows the number of hours in a day for each planet.

Number of Hours in a Day on Different Planets

planet: Earth, Jupiter, Saturn, Neptune, Mars

number of hours: 0 5 10 15 20 25

For more links and activities, go to www.hspscience.com

41

Why Does the Moon Seem to Change?

Fast Fact

The light we see from the moon really comes from the sun. You can make a model to show how this happens.

Why the Moon Seems to Shine

You need

● **foam ball**   ● **foil**   ● **craft stick**   ● **flashlight**

Step 1

Work with a partner. Wrap foil around a ball to **make a model** of the moon. Use a craft stick to make a handle.

Step 2

Hold the handle. Observe the ball in the dark. What does it look like? Shine the flashlight on the ball. What does it look like now?

Step 3

Communicate the effect the light had on the ball.

Inquiry Skill

You can **make a model** to show how something happens.

Reading in Science

VOCABULARY
moon

 READING FOCUS SKILL

CAUSE AND EFFECT Look for the cause of the changes in the way you see the moon.

The Moon Shapes You See

The **moon** is a huge ball of rock that moves in an orbit around Earth. It takes nearly one month for the moon to orbit, or travel around, Earth.

On many nights, the moon seems to shine brightly. But the moon does not give off light of its own, as stars do. It reflects light from the sun.

full moon

first quarter moon

new moon

The moon is always orbiting Earth. So, the part you see of its lighted side changes each night. This makes it seem as if the moon's shape changes.

The phases, or shapes, you see, change as the moon moves. The changes follow a pattern that repeats about every 29 days.

Insta-Lab

Model Moon Phases

Wrap a ball in foil. Hold the ball while a partner shines a light onto it. Slowly turn in place, keeping the ball in front of you. When do you see the new moon, quarter moons, and full moon?

Focus Skill **CAUSE AND EFFECT** What happens when the moon moves around Earth?

last quarter moon

crescent moon

Phases of the Moon

The moon moves one-fourth of the way around Earth in a little more than seven days. Use the pictures to see how the moon moves. About how long does it take the moon to move halfway around Earth? How does its shape seem to change? What happens after about 29 days?

crescent moon

first quarter moon

last quarter moon

full moon

For more links and activities, go to
www.hspscience.com

1. CAUSE AND EFFECT Copy and complete this chart. Tell the effect of each cause.

cause	effect
The sun shines on the moon.	→ The moon reflects **A** _____.
The moon moves around Earth.	→ The moon's shape seems to **B** _____.
The part we see of the moon's lighted side is the same about every 29 days.	→ The moon's phases follow a **C** _____.

2. SUMMARIZE Write two sentences that tell what this lesson is mostly about.

3. VOCABULARY Explain why the **moon** seems to give off light.

Test Prep

4. Which happens about every 29 days?
- **A.** The moon orbits Earth.
- **B.** The moon orbits the sun.
- **C.** The moon gets bigger.
- **D.** The moon gets smaller.

Links

Art

Make a Calendar

Make a blank calendar. Go outside each night for one month, and observe the moon. Draw what you see. Label the new, first quarter, full, and last quarter moon. How many days are there between the phases?

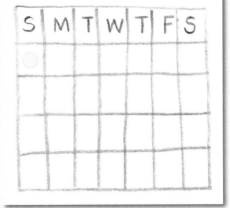

 For more links and activities, go to www.hspscience.com

What Causes the Seasons?

Fast Fact

When North America has summer, South America has winter. You can communicate other facts about the seasons.

Earth's Tilt

You need

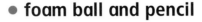

- foam ball and pencil
- lamp

Step 1

Move the ball so that the pencil tip is tilted away from the lamp. Where on the ball does the light shine most brightly?

Step 2

Move the ball to the other side of the lamp. Do not change the pencil's direction or tilt. Where does the light shine most brightly?

Step 3

Communicate what you observe.

Inquiry Skill

When you **communicate** your ideas, you tell or show others what you know.

SI-6 Use observations; **SI-10** Communicate explanations

49

VOCABULARY
season

 READING FOCUS SKILL

CAUSE AND EFFECT Look for the cause of the seasons.

Earth's Orbit Around the Sun

It takes about 365 days for Earth to complete one orbit around the sun. Those 365 days make up Earth's year.

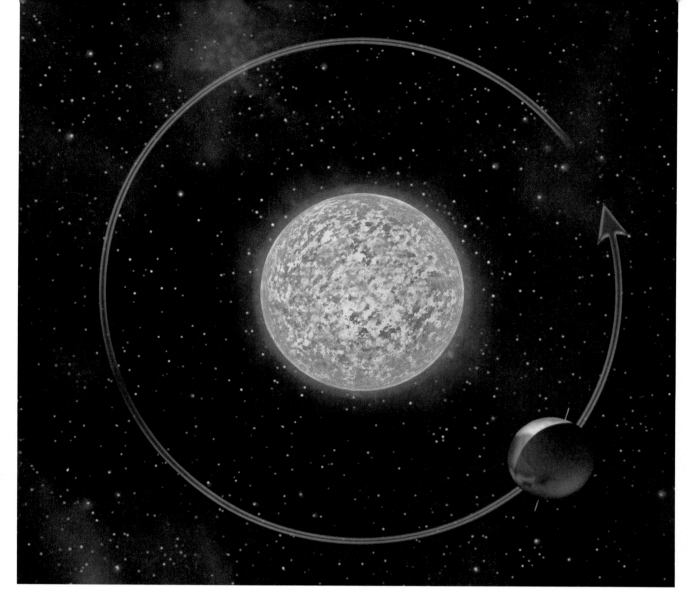

▲ Earth is tilted as it orbits the sun.

Earth is always tilted in the same direction. But the part that is tilted toward the sun changes as Earth orbits the sun. At one time of the year, the northern part of Earth is tilted toward the sun. At other times of the year, it is tilted away from the sun.

CAUSE AND EFFECT Why is one part of Earth sometimes tilted toward the sun and sometimes tilted away from the sun?

Seasons Change

The part of Earth that is tilted toward the sun changes as Earth orbits the sun. This causes the seasons to change.

spring

summer

A **season** is a time of the year that has a certain kind of weather. Spring, summer, fall, and winter are seasons. They repeat in the same pattern each year.

⭐ (Focus Skill) **CAUSE AND EFFECT** What causes the seasons to change?

winter

fall

Why Seases Change

When the part of Earth where you live is tilted toward the sun, it is summer. Sunlight hits that part of Earth directly. This causes warmer temperatures. There are more hours of daylight.

When the part of Earth where you live is tilted away from the sun, it is winter. Sunlight hits that part of Earth at a slant. This causes cooler temperatures. There are fewer hours of daylight.

Insta-Lab

Slanting Light

Shine a flashlight directly onto a sheet of paper. Now tilt the paper so that the light hits it at a slant. Tell what looks different about the light on the paper.

CAUSE AND EFFECT What happens when a part of Earth is tilted toward the sun?

Which day has the most hours of daylight? Why?

Hours of Daylight in Michigan

day	number of hours of daylight
March 21	(bar to ~12)
June 21	(bar to ~15)
September 21	(bar to ~12)
December 21	(bar to ~8)

0 1 2 3 4 5 6 7 8 9 10 11 12 13 14 15

number of hours of daylight

1. CAUSE AND EFFECT Copy and complete this chart. Tell the effect of each cause.

cause

Part of Earth is tilted toward the sun.

Part of Earth is tilted away from the sun.

effect

Temperatures are **A** _____. There are **B** _____ hours of daylight.

That part has **C** _____. Temperatures are **D** _____. There are **E** _____ hours of daylight.

2. DRAW CONCLUSIONS As summer changes to fall, will there be more or fewer hours of daylight? How do you know?

3. VOCABULARY How do the **seasons** form a pattern?

Test Prep

4. Why do the seasons change?

Writing

Sentences About Seasons
Write about Earth's tilt at the beginning of each season where you live. Draw pictures to show the tilt in each season.

Seasons

 For more links and activities, go to **www.hspscience.com**

ST-3 Predict technology effects; **SI-7** Use scientific equipment and tools; **SK-3** Describe effects of science on people

An Assistant in Space

Scientists are building a robot that talks and floats. It will help astronauts in space. The robot is called the Personal Satellite Assistant (PSA).

A Floating Clipboard

One scientist calls the PSA "a floating, talking clipboard." The PSA will have taped information and play it for astronauts. It could tell astronauts how to complete a job.

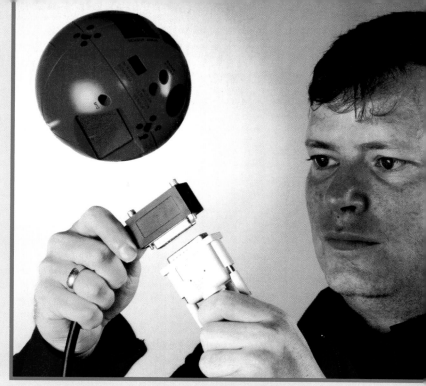

The robot comes with a light and a camera. It can talk to other computers aboard the International Space Station. The PSA may also help keep astronauts safe. The PSA could explore areas for astronauts. It could then tell astronauts the temperature of the area and what the air is like. That way, astronauts would know whether it would be safe for humans to explore an area.

Scientists plan to test the PSA aboard a future space shuttle flight. If the tests go well, the PSA might soon be used aboard the space station.

Think About It

If you had a PSA, how would you use it?

Coming Attractions

Scientists got the idea for the PSA from the movie *Star Wars*. Instead of training a Jedi knight, the softball-sized PSA will give astronauts a helping hand.

Spin-In
Find out more! Log on to
www.hspscience.com

A First Into Space

◄ Ellen Ochoa

In 1991, Ellen Ochoa became the first Latina astronaut. Astronaut Ochoa has been in space four times. She has spent almost 1,000 hours in space.

The longest trip to space for Ellen Ochoa was an 11-day trip in 1999. Together, she and her crew delivered supplies for the first astronauts who were going to live in the International Space Station.

Make a Sundial

What to Do

1. Place the end of the stick in the ground, pointing straight up.

2. When it is 1:00, place one stone at the end of the stick's shadow. Place two stones at 2:00, three stones at 3:00, and so on. Do not move the stones or the stick.

3. Use the stones and the stick's shadow to tell the time the next day.

Materials
- stick
- small stones

Draw Conclusions

Why does the shadow move? Why can the stones be used to tell time the next day?

Temperature Pattern

How do temperatures change from season to season? Find out the usual monthly temperatures where you live. Make a line graph. What patterns do you see? Communicate your observations.

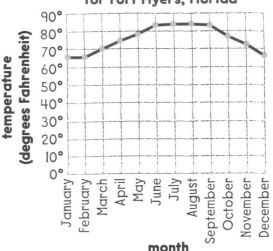

Usual Monthly Temperatures for Fort Myers, Florida

temperature (degrees Fahrenheit): 90° 80° 70° 60° 50° 40° 30° 20° 10° 0°

month: January, February, March, April, May, June, July, August, September, October, November, December

ES-2 Describe motion of sun, moon, stars; **ES-4** Describe weather changes; **ES-5** Measure weather; **SI-6** Use observations; **SI-7** Use scientific equipment and tools; **SI-8** Measure properties; **SI-9** Use numbers; **SI-10** Communicate explanations

59

Review and Test Preparation

Vocabulary Review

Use the terms below to complete the sentences. The page numbers tell you where to look if you need help.

solar system p. 32 **star** p. 34
planet p. 32 **constellation** p. 34
orbit p. 33 **rotate** p. 38

1. A path around something is an _____.

2. A huge ball of hot gases is a _____.

3. To spin around is to _____.

4. The sun, all its planets, and the planets' moons make up the _____.

5. A large ball of rock or gas that moves around the sun is a _____.

6. A group of stars that forms a pattern is a _____.

Check Understanding

7. When are the stars and planets in the sky?

    A. only in the morning

    B. only at night

    C. only in the afternoon

    D. all the time

8. Which detail about Earth's rotation is correct?

    F. It causes the sun to move.

    G. It causes winter to become spring.

    H. It causes Earth to have day and night.

    J. It causes summer to become fall.

Critical Thinking

9. What would happen if Earth were not tilted as it orbits?

10. Why don't all parts of Earth have light at the same time?

Chapter 2

Weather

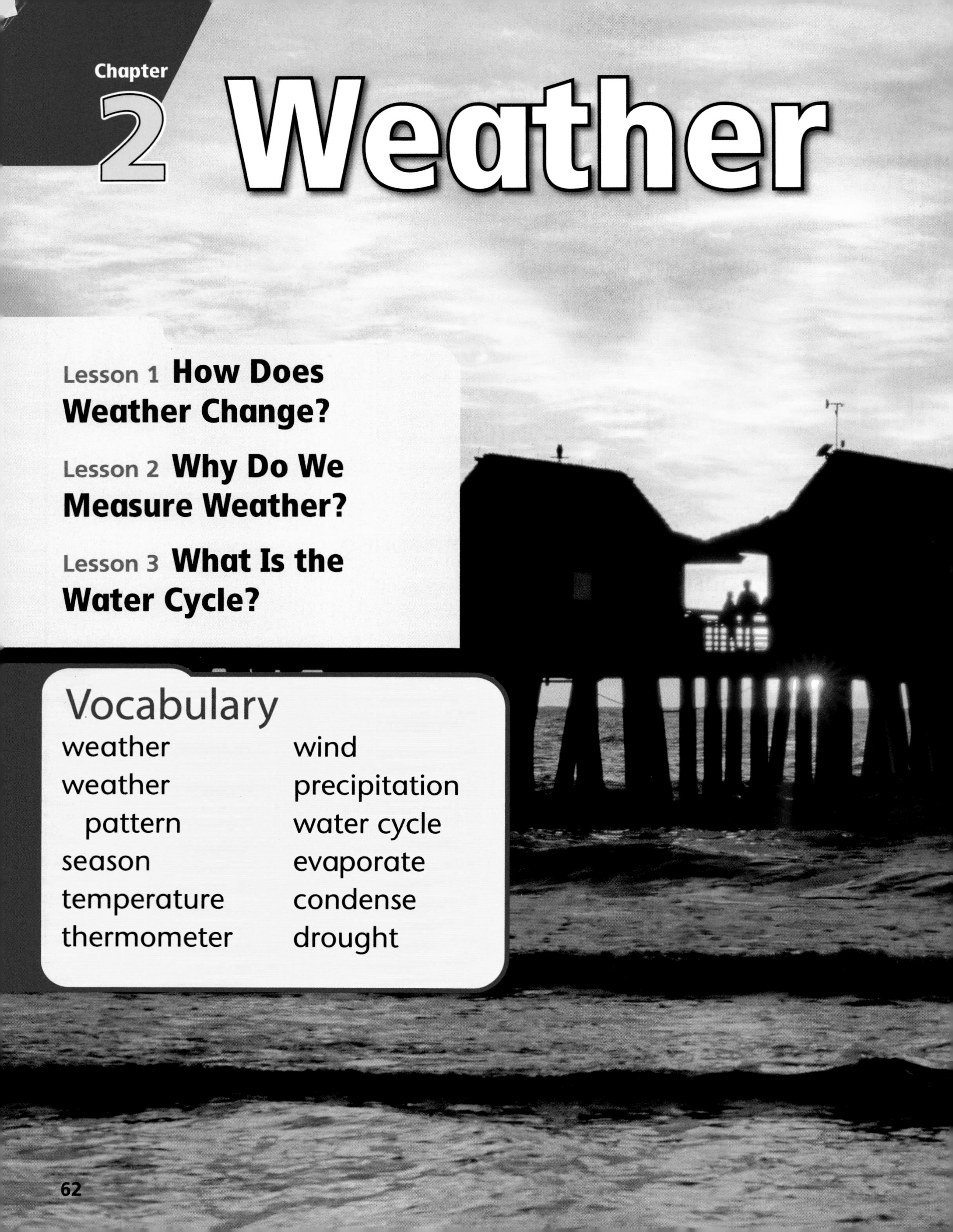

Lesson 1 **How Does Weather Change?**

Lesson 2 **Why Do We Measure Weather?**

Lesson 3 **What Is the Water Cycle?**

Vocabulary

weather
weather pattern
season
temperature
thermometer
wind
precipitation
water cycle
evaporate
condense
drought

I wonder...

How do people know what the weather is going to be?

What do you wonder?

63

How Does Weather Change?

Fast Fact

It takes both light and water to make a rainbow. You may see a rainbow if the sun shines while it is raining or right after the rain stops. By observing the weather, you can see its patterns.

Changes in Weather

You need

- poster board
- markers

Step 1

Make up a symbol to stand for each kind of weather. Then draw a chart like this one.

Weather
Monday
Tuesday
Wednesday
Thursday
Friday

Step 2

Observe the weather each day for 5 days. Record what you **observed**.

Step 3

What kinds of weather did you **observe**? Share your information.

Inquiry Skill

Observing weather helps you see how it changes. It also helps you see weather patterns.

VOCABULARY

weather
weather pattern
season

 READING FOCUS SKILL

SEQUENCE Look for the order of seasons and the ways the weather changes from one season to the next.

Weather

What is the weather like today? Is it hot or cold? Is it rainy, snowy, sunny, cloudy, or windy? **Weather** is what the air outside is like. It can change in just a few hours or over many months. A change in the weather that repeats is called a **weather pattern**.

 SEQUENCE What usually happens after it rains?

Spring

A **season** is a time of year that has a certain kind of weather. In many places, the weather changes with each season. In spring, the air gets warmer. In some places, it is very rainy in spring. As the weather gets warmer and wetter, plants begin to grow.

(Focus Skill) **SEQUENCE** How does the air change in spring?

Insta-Lab

Model a Rainbow

Place a mirror in a jar of water. Make the room dark. Shine a flashlight on the mirror. Move the light around. Shine it from different directions until you see rainbow colors.

Summer

Summer comes after spring. In most places, summer is the warmest time of year. The days are often hot and sunny. But storms can quickly change the weather. In summer, trees and other plants have many leaves.

SEQUENCE Which season comes before summer?

Fall

Fall is the next season. In fall, the air gets cooler. Some fall days are sunny, while others are cloudy. In fall, the leaves of some trees change color and then drop off. Some plants stop growing and die.

⭐ **Focus Skill** **SEQUENCE** How may trees change from summer to fall?

Winter

After fall, winter comes. This is the coldest season. In some places, it gets cold enough to snow. In these places, many trees and bushes have no leaves until spring.

In other places, the air cools down just a little. It may never be cold enough to snow there. Many trees and plants keep their leaves. Many flowers keep growing.

Spring comes again after winter. The pattern of changing seasons goes on.

SEQUENCE What happens to many trees when winter ends?

1. SEQUENCE Copy and complete this chart. Tell about each season in order.

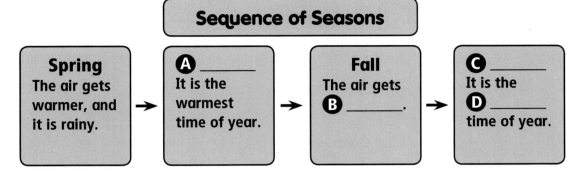

Sequence of Seasons

| **Spring** The air gets warmer, and it is rainy. | → | **A** _____ It is the warmest time of year. | → | **Fall** The air gets **B** _____. | → | **C** _____ It is the **D** _____ time of year. |

2. SUMMARIZE Write a summary of the lesson. Begin with the sentence **Weather can change with the seasons.**

3. VOCABULARY Describe how **weather patterns** change from summer to fall.

Test Prep

4. How can you tell it is spring?
   A. Trees have no leaves.
   B. Trees grow new leaves.
   C. Some leaves change color.
   D. Trees have lots of leaves.

Links

Writing

Weather Report
Choose a season. Write a short weather report for one day of that season in Ohio and in another state. Present your weather report. Use a map to point out the two states.

For more links and activities, go to www.hspscience.com

71

Why Do We Measure Weather?

The coldest temperature ever measured in the United States was recorded in Alaska on January 23, 1971. You can compare temperatures to see how the weather changes.

Measure Temperature

You need

● **thermometer**

Make a chart like this one.

Temperature	
Morning	
Noon	
Late Afternoon	

Read the thermometer in the morning, at noon, and in the late afternoon. Record each temperature.

Compare the temperatures.

Inquiry Skill

Comparing temperatures helps you see a pattern of temperature change.

ES-4 Describe weather changes; **ES-5** Measure weather; **ST-2** Investigate how technology meets needs; **SI-6** Use observations; **SI-7** Use scientific equipment and tools; **SI-8** Measure properties; **SI-9** Use numbers

73

Reading in Science

ES-4 Describe weather changes; ES-5 Measure weather; ST-2 Investigate how technology meets needs; SI-8 Measure properties; SI-9 Use numbers

VOCABULARY

temperature
thermometer
wind
precipitation

 READING FOCUS SKILL

MAIN IDEA AND DETAILS Look for details that tell why and how weather is measured.

Measuring Weather

Scientists use tools to measure the weather. Some tools tell how warm the air is. Some tools tell how fast the wind is blowing. Other tools tell how much rain has fallen.

Measuring weather helps scientists see patterns. Patterns help the scientists predict the weather. Then they can tell people how to get ready for the weather.

 MAIN IDEA AND DETAILS How do scientists measure weather?

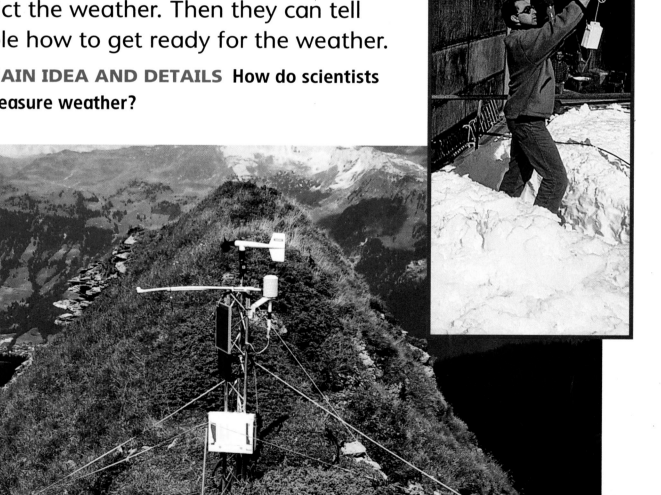

74

Measuring Temperature

Temperature is the measure of how warm something is. A tool called a **thermometer** is used to measure temperature. Scientists use thermometers to record the temperature of the air. Warm air makes the liquid in some thermometers go up. Cool air makes the liquid go down.

▲ Which thermometer shows the temperature for a cold day?

MAIN IDEA AND DETAILS How can you use a thermometer to learn about the weather?

Measuring Wind

Wind is moving air. It can move in different directions. Scientists use a weather vane to find out which way the wind is blowing. The wind turns the arrow on the vane. The arrow points to the direction the wind is coming from.

Insta-Lab

Draw and Compare

Look outside. Is the wind blowing? How can you tell? Draw a picture that shows what the wind is doing. Use the pictures on the next page to tell about the wind's speed.

Scientists measure the speed of wind with a tool called an anemometer.

You can use the pictures on this page to estimate wind speed. They show the effects of wind at different speeds. The wind speeds are measured in miles per hour.

▲ anemometer

 MAIN IDEA AND DETAILS
What tools measure wind? What do they help you learn?

Effects of Wind at Different Speeds

0–1 mile

1–3 miles

8–12 miles

25–31 miles

32–38 miles

64–75 miles

Measuring Precipitation

Water that falls from the sky is called **precipitation**. Rain, snow, sleet, and hail are kinds of precipitation.

Scientists use a rain gauge to find out how much rain falls. This container catches rain. Then scientists can measure how many inches of rain fell. You can use a ruler and a jar to make your own rain gauge.

⭐ *Focus Skill* **MAIN IDEA AND DETAILS** What is precipitation? What are kinds of precipitation?

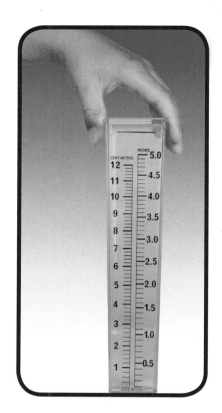

rain gauge ▲

1. MAIN IDEA AND DETAILS Copy and complete this chart. Tell about the weather tools scientists use.

Main Idea and Details

Scientists use tools to measure weather.

A **A** _____ measures how much rain falls.

An anemometer measures the speed of the **B** _____.

A **C** _____ shows the direction of the wind.

A **D** _____ measures the temperature of the air.

2. DRAW CONCLUSIONS Why is it important to measure weather?

3. VOCABULARY Use the term **precipitation** to tell about this picture.

Test Prep

4. How do scientists learn about weather?

Links

Math

Make a Bar Graph

Rainfall changes from month to month. This chart shows the rainfall in Tampa, Florida, for four different months. Use the data to make a bar graph. What can you tell from your graph?

Tampa, Florida

Month	Rainfall
April	2 inches
May	3 inches
September	7 inches
October	2 inches

For more links and activities, go to **www.hspscience.com**

What Is the Water Cycle?

Fast Fact

Water is in lakes, rivers, and oceans. It is also in the air. You know that water falls as rain or snow from the air into bodies of water. You can infer how water gets into the air.

Water in the Air

You need

- 2 zip-top bags
- colored water
- tape

Step 1

Fill each bag halfway with water. Zip the bags closed.

Step 2

Tape one bag to a window in the sun. Tape the other bag to a window in the shade.

Step 3

Wait 30 minutes. Then observe both bags. Record what you observe. Which bag shows more change? Infer what caused the change.

Inquiry Skill

When you infer, you use what you see to figure out what happened.

ES-4 Describe weather changes; **SI-6** Use observations

Reading in Science

VOCABULARY

water cycle
evaporate
condense
drought

(Focus Skill) **READING FOCUS SKILL**

CAUSE AND EFFECT Look for causes and effects as you read about the water cycle.

The Water Cycle

Water moves over and over again from Earth's surface into the air and then back to Earth's surface. This movement of water is called the **water cycle**.

 CAUSE AND EFFECT What makes water move from Earth into the air?

 **Science Up Close**

What Happens During the Water Cycle

3 The water vapor cools and **condenses**, or changes into tiny drops of water.

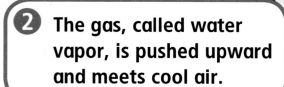

2 The gas, called water vapor, is pushed upward and meets cool air.

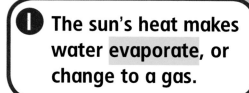

1 The sun's heat makes water **evaporate**, or change to a gas.

82

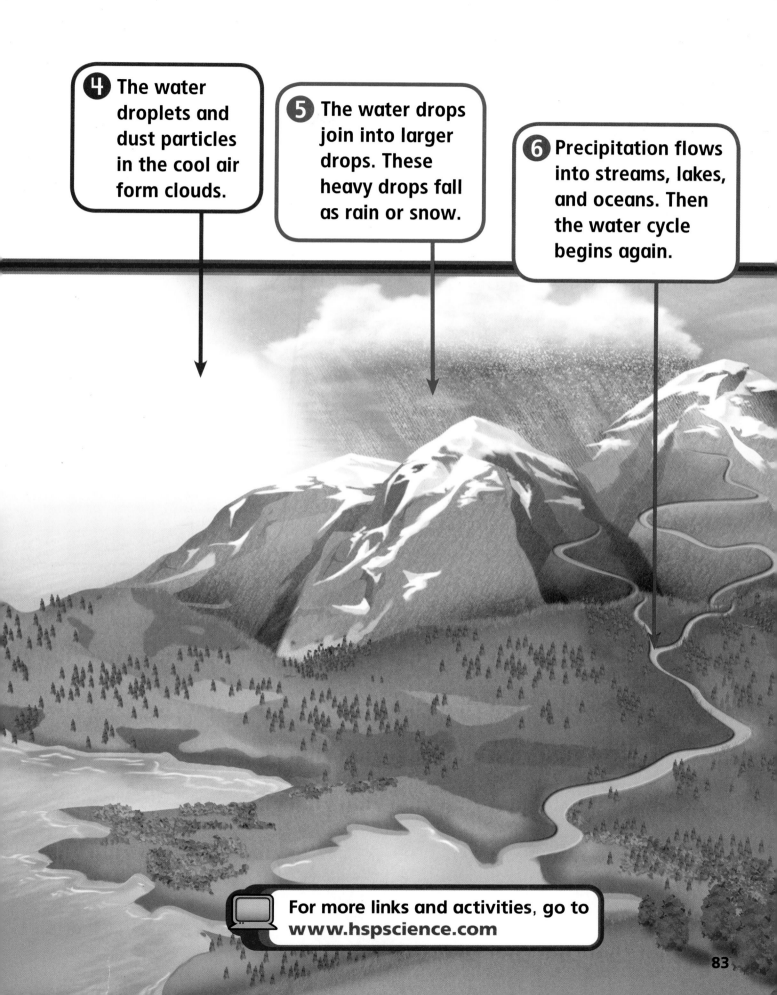

4 The water droplets and dust particles in the cool air form clouds.

5 The water drops join into larger drops. These heavy drops fall as rain or snow.

6 Precipitation flows into streams, lakes, and oceans. Then the water cycle begins again.

For more links and activities, go to www.hspscience.com

Droughts

Sometimes it does not rain for a long time. This time is called a **drought**. The weather may be hotter than usual. The land may get very dry, and streams and ponds may dry up. Winds may blow away the soil.

Without water, plants and animals may die. People have to use very little water when there is a drought.

▲ corn plants harmed by a drought

 CAUSE AND EFFECT What can happen because of a drought?

Floods

If a lot of rain falls, it can cause a flood. Rivers and streams overflow. Some land is covered with water.

Too much water can kill plants and animals. People must get to safe, dry places when there is a flood.

CAUSE AND EFFECT What can happen because of a flood?

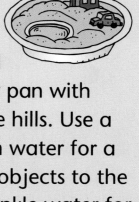

Insta-Lab

Model a Flood

Fill a shallow pan with soil. Shape some hills. Use a jar lid filled with water for a lake. Add small objects to the scene. Then sprinkle water for rain until you model a flood. Share your results.

Storms

Storms are a kind of weather that can be harmful. A thunderstorm has rain, thunder, and lightning. The rain from the storm may cause a flood. Lightning may strike trees and other tall things.

When it is cold, a lot of snow may fall. A snowstorm with strong winds is called a blizzard. The blowing snow makes it hard to see. Stay indoors to keep safe in thunderstorms and snowstorms.

(Focus Skill) CAUSE AND EFFECT **Why are some storms harmful?**

86

1. CAUSE AND EFFECT Copy and complete this chart. Write an effect for each cause.

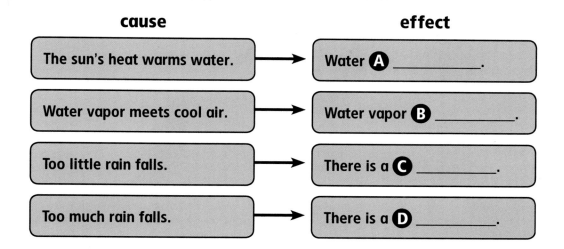

cause	effect
The sun's heat warms water.	Water **A** _____.
Water vapor meets cool air.	Water vapor **B** _____.
Too little rain falls.	There is a **C** _____.
Too much rain falls.	There is a **D** _____.

2. SUMMARIZE Use the vocabulary to write a summary of the lesson.

3. VOCABULARY Explain what happens during the **water cycle**.

Test Prep

4. It has not rained for a long time. It is hot, and the soil is dry. What is this time called?
 A. a flood
 B. a blizzard
 C. a drought
 D. a thunderstorm

Links

Art

Water Cycle Poster
Make a poster to show the water cycle. On your poster, label the parts of the water cycle.

 For more links and activities, go to **www.hspscience.com**

SCIENCE Spin from WEEKLY READER®

Technology

LS-2 Identify environments;
LS-6 Investigate plant/
animal adaptations; ST-1 Explain
technology benefits/risks;
ST-2 Investigate how technology
meets needs

The Coldest Place on Earth

Experts say that Antarctica is the coldest place on Earth. But if it's that cold, how do animals and people stay warm there?

Cold Weather, Warm Penguins

Penguins are birds that live in Antarctica. They have feathers that are very small and close together. The feathers have oil on them. Cold water can't get through the feathers to touch the penguins' skin. A layer of fat under their skin helps keep the penguins warm, too.

Weddell seals also live in Antarctica. They swim in the icy ocean to catch fish and other food. Like penguins, Weddell seals stay warm because they have a layer of blubber, or fat, under their skin. A coat of thick fur keeps the cold water from touching the seals' skin.

Playful Penguin Facts

* Penguins can waddle faster than humans can walk.

* Penguins line up and dive into the water again and again.

* Penguins sometimes toboggan, or slide, on their bellies.

* Penguins surf waves to get back to shore.

Keeping People Warm

Scientists who work in Antarctica have learned from the animals. When they are outside, scientists stay warm the same way the animals do. They wear layers of clothing that trap their body heat. Over these clothes, they wear a parka. The parka is made of special materials that have been developed to keep the cold air from touching the scientists' skin.

Think About It

What are some other things people have learned from observing animals?

Spin In

Find out more! Log on to
www.hspscience.com

What's the Weather?

Willow Wilaszek lives in Alaska. The Peninsula Winter Games are played in Alaska. The games are played mostly outdoors. Willow and other children enjoy playing the games.

What does Willow know about winter weather? She knows that she must wear extra clothes because of the very cold temperatures every winter. Before she plays outside in winter, she puts on the clothes she needs to keep her warm.

How Water Vapor Condenses

You need
- 2 metal cans • ice water
- warm water

What to Do

1. Fill one can halfway with ice water.
2. Fill the other can halfway with warm water.
3. Wait five minutes. Then look at the outside of each can. Record changes you observe.

Draw Conclusions

Are the cans different on the outside? How? Why did the changes happen?

What Is the Temperature?

Does the temperature outside stay the same from day to day? Use a thermometer to check the temperature every day at the same time. Use your data to make a graph. What pattern do you see? Share the graph with your class.

Temperature at 10:00

Monday	
Tuesday	
Wednesday	
Thursday	
Friday	

 ES-4 Describe weather changes; **ES-5** Measure weather; **SI-6** Use observations; **SI-7** Use scientific equipment and tools; **SI-8** Measure properties; **SI-9** Use numbers; **SI-10** Communicate explanations

Review and Test Preparation

Vocabulary Review

Use the terms to complete the sentences.
The page numbers tell you where to look
if you need help.

weather pattern p. 66   **precipitation** p. 78
thermometer p. 75   **water cycle** p. 82

1. Rain, snow, and sleet are kinds
of _____.

2. The movement of water from Earth's
surface into the air and back is
the _____.

3. A weather change that repeats is
a _____.

4. One tool that measures the weather is
a _____.

Check Understanding

5. Put these seasons in the
(Focus Skill) correct sequence.

spring   fall   summer   winter

6. Think about weather patterns. Write about the four seasons. Tell what each season's weather is like.

7. How are these tools alike?

A. Both measure rainfall.
B. Both measure temperature.
C. Both measure weather.
D. Both measure wind.

Critical Thinking

8. Think about the water cycle. Explain what will happen to a puddle when the sun comes out.

9. Write about three tools a scientist could use to learn about a thunderstorm.

Columbus

Cincinnati

Drake Planetarium

Drake Planetarium in Cincinnati presents a show that is "out of this world"!

The Drake Planetarium is a big, round room shaped like an upside-down bowl. On its round ceiling, you can see a sky show. This is possible because of a machine called the star projector.

Drake Planetarium

sky show

The star projector makes the sky show. Inside the machine is a bright light. A plate with small holes covers the light. When it is dark in the room, the light shines through the small holes. This makes little spots on the dome that look like stars at night. The "stars" are in the same places as the real stars in the sky.

planets and stars

Think and Do

1. **SCIENCE AND TECHNOLOGY** Scientists use powerful telescopes to help them see the stars at night. How do telescopes help scientists find and study stars? Describe your ideas with words and pictures.

2. **SCIENTIFIC THINKING** How many stars are in the sky? Try this. With an adult family member, go outside one evening and try to count all the stars. The two of you might try counting the stars in different areas. Discuss what you find out.

ES-1 Recognize that there are too many stars to count; **ST-2** Investigate how technology meets needs; **SK-3** Describe effects of science on people and environment

95

Caesar Creek State Park
Columbus

Animals of Ancient Ohio

Did you know that Ohio is one of the best places in the world to find fossils? One great place to hunt for them is near Waynesville, Ohio. It is Caesar Creek State Park. There you can find fossils of some of Ohio's earliest animals.

Most fossils are found in very old rocks. That is why fossil hunting is good in this park. It has some of the oldest rocks in Ohio.

In these rocks, you can find the state fossil of Ohio. It looks like a huge bug. You can also find smaller fossils of animals that look like marbles.

very old seashells

Scientists use tools to help them look for fossils.

Think and Do

I. SCIENTIFIC THINKING Look on a map to find the place in Ohio where you live. Use media center resources to find out what kinds of fossils can be found near where you live. Choose one of these, draw a picture of it, and write a description.

2. SCIENTIFIC THINKING Draw pictures of tools that might be useful to a scientist who is looking for fossils. Write words or sentences to communicate why these tools would be helpful.

Milligan — Columbus

Weather Tour

Did you ever say, "Today must be the coldest day ever?" It may have felt that way, but it probably was not the coldest day.

Ohio's winters are cold and dry, but very cold weather is not common. However, on February 10, 1899, the temperature dropped to −39°F. in Milligan, Ohio. This is the coldest temperature ever recorded in Ohio.

Cold air sweeps down from Canada. There are no mountains to stop the cold air.

It's cold!

Summers in Ohio can be hot. One day in 1897, the temperature went up to 113°F! It happened again on July 21, 1934, in Thurman, Ohio.

It's hot!

Think and Do

1. **SCIENCE AND TECHNOLOGY** Some people need to know what the air temperature is for their job. Choose one career, and explain why it is important for a person with this job to know the air temperature.

2. **SCIENTIFIC THINKING** Look back at the coldest and hottest temperatures recorded in Ohio. Draw a line down the middle of a sheet of paper. Write <u>Hot</u> on one side and <u>Cold</u> on the other. Then draw pictures and write words to communicate how you would prepare for each type of weather.

ES-4 Describe weather changes: **ES-5** Measure weather; **SI-10** Communicate explanations; **SK-3** Describe effects of science on people

99

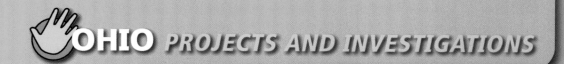

First Star I See Tonight

Materials
- star chart
- paper
- pencil

What to Do

1. Find some star charts in a book or online.

2. Find star patterns you want to look for in the sky. Make a list of them.

3. With an adult family member, go outside at night. Look for these star patterns. When you find them, cross them off your list.

4. Go outside at a different time each night for one week. See if the stars are in the same places.

5. Record your observations.

Draw Conclusions

1. Which star patterns were the easiest to find? Which were the hardest?

2. Were the stars in the same place each night? Why do you think that happens?

Temperature Watch

Materials
- outdoor thermometer
- chart paper
- drawing paper
- colored pencils

What to Do

1. Observe the weather each day in the morning and in the evening.

2. Record your data in a chart. Also draw a picture of the weather when you took each temperature. Was it sunny? Rainy? Cloudy? Foggy?

3. Compare your findings. Which day was the coldest? Which day was the warmest? How did the weather change during each day?

Draw Conclusions

1. Why do you think the temperature changed each day?

2. How many times was the morning weather different from the evening weather? Why do you think that happens?

ES-2 Describe motion of sun, moon, stars; **ES-4** Describe weather changes; **ES-5** Measure weather; **SI-5** Explain outcomes; **SI-6** Use observations

101

UNIT B

Cleveland Holden Arboretum

⊙ Columbus

Life Sciences

The chapters and features in this unit address these Grade Level Indicators from the Ohio Academic Content Standards for Science.

Chapter 3 Living Things and Their Environments

LS-1   Explain that animals, including people, need air, water, food, living space and shelter; plants need air, water, nutrients (e.g., minerals), living space and light to survive.

LS-2   Identify that there are many distinct environments that support different kinds of organisms.

LS-3   Explain why organisms can survive only in environments that meet their needs (e.g., organisms that once lived on Earth have disappeared for different reasons such as natural forces or human-caused effects).

LS-4   Compare similarities and differences among individuals of the same kind of plants and animals, including people.

LS-6   Investigate the different structures of plants and animals that help them live in different environments (e.g., lungs, gills, leaves and roots).

Chapter 4 Living Things Need Energy

LS-5   Explain that food is a basic need of plants and animals (e.g., plants need sunlight to make food and to grow, animals eat plants and/or other animals for food, food chain) and is important because it is a source of energy (e.g., energy used to play, ride bicycles, read, etc.).

Chapter 5 Living Things in Ohio

LS-7   Compare the habitats of many different kinds of Ohio plants and animals and some of the ways animals depend on plants and each other.

LS-8   Compare the activities of Ohio's common animals (e.g., squirrels, chipmunks, deer, butterflies, bees, ants, bats and frogs) during the different seasons by describing changes in their behaviors and body covering.

LS-9   Compare Ohio plants during the different seasons by describing changes in their appearance.

Unit B Ohio Expeditions

The investigations and experiences in this unit also address many of the Grade Level Indicators for standards in Science and Technology, Scientific Inquiry, and Scientific Ways of Knowing.

TO: maryalice@hspscience.com
FROM: plantgal@hspscience.com
RE: Cleveland Holden Arboretum

Dear Mary Alice,

Today I went to the largest tree garden in the country! Cleveland Holden Arboretum is a very cool place. I learned where plants get their names. Did you know that the word <u>fern</u> means "feathers"? The leaves of a fern really do look like feathers!

Plants rock!
Lynnette

Experiment!

Plants and Light

How does light change the way a plant grows? Plan and do a test to find out.

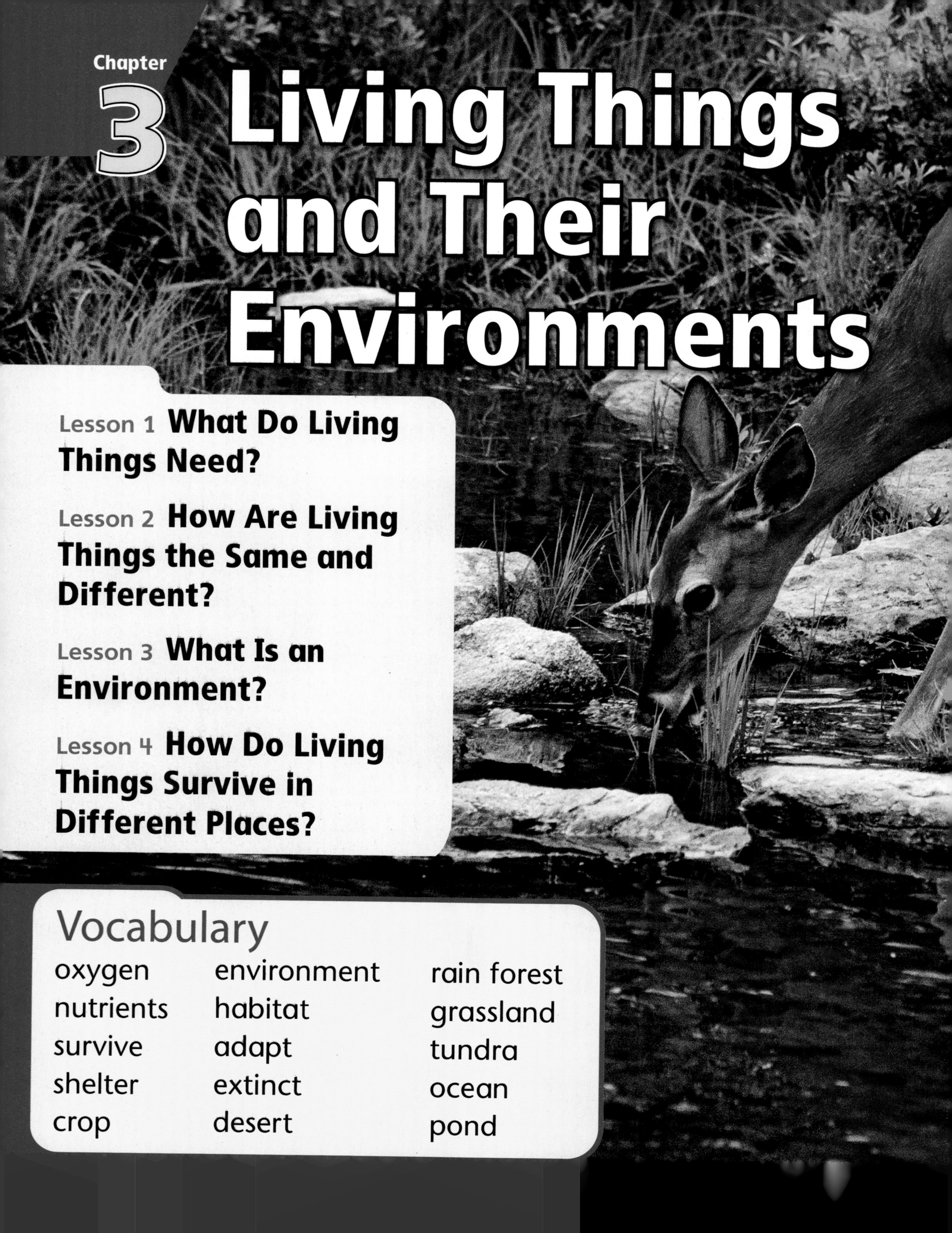

Living Things and Their Environments

Vocabulary

oxygen	environment	rain forest
nutrients	habitat	grassland
survive	adapt	tundra
shelter	extinct	ocean
crop	desert	pond

I wonder...

What do living things need?

What do **you** wonder?

What Do Living Things Need?

Fast Fact

There are more than 300,000 kinds of plants. They all need the same things to live. Knowing the things all plants need helps you predict what will happen to plants that do not get them.

What Plants Need to Grow

You need

- 2 plants
- cup of water

Step 1

Put both plants in a sunny place. Water only one plant. Put labels on the plants. **Predict** what will happen.

Step 2

Make a chart like this one.

Plant with water	Plant with no water

Step 3

Observe both plants every day. Water only one plant. Record any changes. Was your **prediction** correct?

Inquiry Skill

When you **predict**, you use what you know to say what you think will happen.

LS-1 Explore organisms' basic needs; LS-5 Explain need for food; SI-5 Explain outcomes; SI-6 Use observations

Reading in Science

 LS-1 Explore organisms' basic needs; **LS-2** Identify environments;
LS-5 Explain need for food, **LS-6** Investigate plant/animal adaptations

VOCABULARY

oxygen
nutrients
survive
shelter

(Focus Skill) **READING FOCUS SKILL**

COMPARE AND CONTRAST Compare what all living things need to survive.

Plants

Plants, animals, and people are living things. Living things need food, water, and oxygen. **Oxygen** is a gas in air and water.

Plants make their own food. They use water, light, and gases in air to make it. They take in nutrients from the ground. **Nutrients** are substances they need to be healthy. Plants need all these things to **survive**, or stay alive.

A cactus grows in a dry desert. ▶

A bald-cypress tree grows in a wet swamp. ▼

Plants also need space to live and grow. As many plants grow, they need more space. The leaves get bigger. The roots and stems get longer. A plant in a small container may need to be moved to a larger one to give it more room to grow.

COMPARE AND CONTRAST How do plants change as they grow?

Animals

Animals need food, oxygen, and water to survive. Bigger animals need more food than smaller ones. Whales and bears need more food than rabbits and owls.

As an animal grows, it needs more food and water. An adult turtle needs more food than a young turtle.

Animals need space. They need room to move around, find food, and care for their young.

Animals also need shelter. A **shelter** is a safe place to live. Prairie dogs dig holes for shelter. There they hide from animals that could eat them. The holes also keep them safe from bad weather. Owls and squirrels use trees for shelter. Some tigers and bears use caves.

COMPARE AND CONTRAST What do all animals need to survive?

Insta-Lab

Clay Nest
Make a nest out of clay. How does a nest help keep eggs and chicks safe?

People

Like animals, people need water, oxygen, and food to survive. They need water to drink. They need oxygen to breathe. They need food to eat.

People also need shelter. They need a safe place to live. They need a place that protects them from bad weather.

COMPARE AND CONTRAST **What different things do people use for shelter?**

1. COMPARE AND CONTRAST Copy and complete the chart. Tell how the needs of living things are alike and different.

Plants, Animals, and People

alike	different
All need food and **A** _____.	Only **B** _____ make their own food.
All need **C** _____ from the air or water.	Only people and **D** _____ need to move around.
	Animals and people need **E** _____ to stay safe.

2. DRAW CONCLUSIONS Why do different kinds of animals need different kinds of shelters?

3. VOCABULARY Where do plants get **nutrients**?

Test Prep

4. What do people need to survive?

Writing

List of Things a Pet Needs
Choose an animal you would like to have as a pet. Draw a picture of it. Then write a list of ways you can help it get the things it needs to survive.

I can give my cat food and water.

 For more links and activities, go to www.hspscience.com

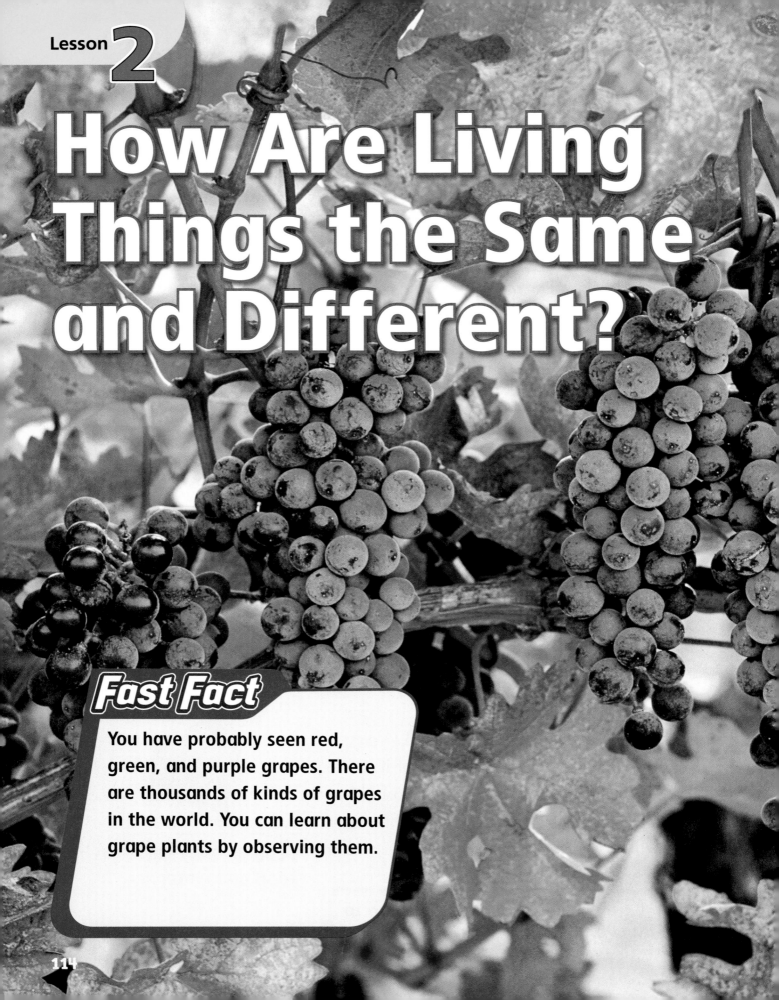

How Are Living Things the Same and Different?

Fast Fact

You have probably seen red, green, and purple grapes. There are thousands of kinds of grapes in the world. You can learn about grape plants by observing them.

Parts of a Plant

You need

- 2 carnations

- 2 clear cups with colored water

Step 1

Bend the stem of one carnation.

Step 2

Put each carnation in a cup of colored water.

Step 3

Observe the carnations for two days. What changes do you see?

Inquiry Skill

You can use your senses of sight, smell, and touch to observe plants.

Reading in Science

LS-1 Explore organisms' basic needs; **LS-4** Compare organisms; **SI-6** Use observations; **SI-9** Use numbers; **SI-10** Communicate explanations; **SK-4** Explain advantages of teamwork

VOCABULARY
crop

 READING FOCUS SKILL

COMPARE AND CONTRAST Look for ways the same kinds of plants and animals are alike and different.

Plants

Plants of the same kind are alike in some ways. Roses are a kind of plant. Roses have roots, stems, leaves, and flowers that are alike.

The same kinds of plants are also different in some ways. Roses are not all the same color, size, and shape. Some plants have more flowers than others.

How are these rose plants alike? How are they different?

Crops are plants that people grow and use. Some crops are used for food. A crop is made up of the same kind of plant. The plants may look alike, but they are not all the same color, size, and shape.

Corn is a crop. How are the corn plants in the pictures the same? How are they different?

⭐ (Focus Skill) **COMPARE AND CONTRAST**
How are the plants in a crop alike?

Compare Apples

Observe 3 apples. How are they alike? Different? Write your observations. Share them with a partner. How is this helpful?

Animals

Animals of the same kind are alike in some ways. Cows are a kind of animal. Cows have a tail, four legs, two eyes, and fur.

The same kinds of animals are also different in some ways. All cows are not the same color and size. Some cows have fur that is one color. Some cows have fur that is many colors. Some cows are bigger than others.

▼ **How are the cows alike and different?**

Chickens are another kind of animal. Chickens have wings, a beak, and feathers. But not all chickens are the same color or size. The parts of their bodies may not be the same shape.

⭐ **COMPARE AND CONTRAST** How are animals of the same kind alike? How are they different?

119

People

All people are the same in some ways and different in other ways. For example, people have two eyes. But some people have blue eyes and others have brown eyes. Some people have straight hair. Others have curly hair.

Look at these children. How are they the same? How are they different?

 COMPARE AND CONTRAST How are people alike and different?

Focus Skill

1. COMPARE AND CONTRAST Copy and complete the chart. Tell how cows are alike and different.

Cows

alike	different
Cows are a kind of **A** _____.	Cows are different colors and **B** _____.
Cows have a tail, ears, and fur.	Some cows have fur that is one color.
	Some cows have fur that is **C**____ colors.

2. SUMMARIZE Write two sentences that tell what this lesson is about.

3. VOCABULARY Use the word **crop** to tell about plants.

Test Prep

4. How are chickens the same?
  A. They all have fur.
  B. They are the same color.
  C. They are the same size.
  D. They all have wings.

Links

Math

Compare Amounts

Different animals need different amounts of food. Use the chart to compare how much food three dogs eat each day. Which eats the most? The least? How much would each dog eat in 3 days?

Dog	Amount of Food
Sandy	1 cup
Rosey	2 cups
Bo	3 cups

For more links and activities, go to www.hspscience.com

121

What Is an Environment?

Fast Fact

Alligators live in lakes, ponds, and rivers. They can hide in the water while they hunt for food. You can draw conclusions to figure out why animals live in certain places.

Where an Animal Lives

You need

● **animal pictures**

● **markers**

Step 1

Choose an animal picture.

Step 2

Draw a picture to show where the animal lives.

Step 3

Draw conclusions about why this is a good place for the animal to live.

Inquiry Skill

You use your observations and what you know to **draw conclusions**.

Reading in Science

 LS-1 Identify organisms' basic needs; **LS-2** Identify environments; **LS-3** Explain need for habitats; **LS-5** Explain need for food; **LS-6** Investigate plant/ animal adaptations; **SI-2** Ask "how do we know" questions; **SI-6** Use observations

VOCABULARY

environment
habitat
adapt
extinct

(Focus Skill) **READING FOCUS SKILL**

MAIN IDEA AND DETAILS Look for details about where animals and plants live.

Environments and Habitats

An **environment** is made up of all the living and nonliving things in a place. Animals and plants are the living things. Water, weather, and rocks are some of the nonliving things. Environments can be hot or cold. They can be wet or dry. Animals and plants from one environment often can not live in another one.

An environment is made up of different habitats. A **habitat** is a place where living things have food and water and the kind of shelter they need. In a forest environment, a pond is a habitat for fish. Part of the forest may be a habitat for birds. What habitats do you see in this picture?

⭐ **MAIN IDEA AND DETAILS**
(Focus Skill) **What do animals and plants need in a habitat?**

▲ sea otters

red pigfish ▶

How Animals and Plants Adapt

Over time, animals and plants **adapt**, or change, to be able to live in their environment. They adapt in different ways to meet their needs. A fish has gills to take in oxygen from water. An otter has fur to keep it warm.

Insta-Lab

How Feathers Help Ducks
Cut out two paper feathers. Cover both sides of one feather with margarine. Dip both feathers into a bowl of water. Which one does not soak up water? Why do you think ducks have an oily coating on their feathers?

Beaks and Teeth

Animals' beaks and teeth are adapted to help them get food.

You can tell what kind of food a bird eats by looking at the shape of its beak.

You can tell what kind of food other animals eat by looking at their teeth.

 MAIN IDEA AND DETAILS **Why do plants and animals adapt?**

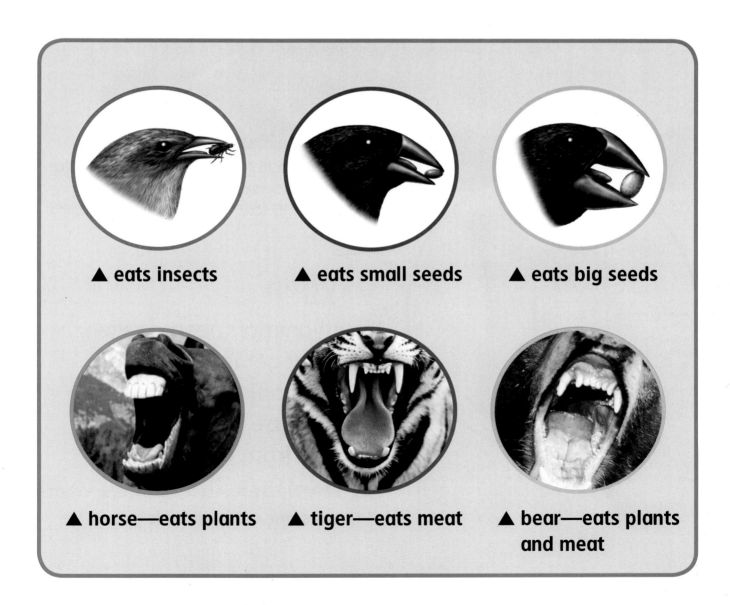

▲ eats insects   ▲ eats small seeds   ▲ eats big seeds

▲ horse—eats plants   ▲ tiger—eats meat   ▲ bear—eats plants and meat

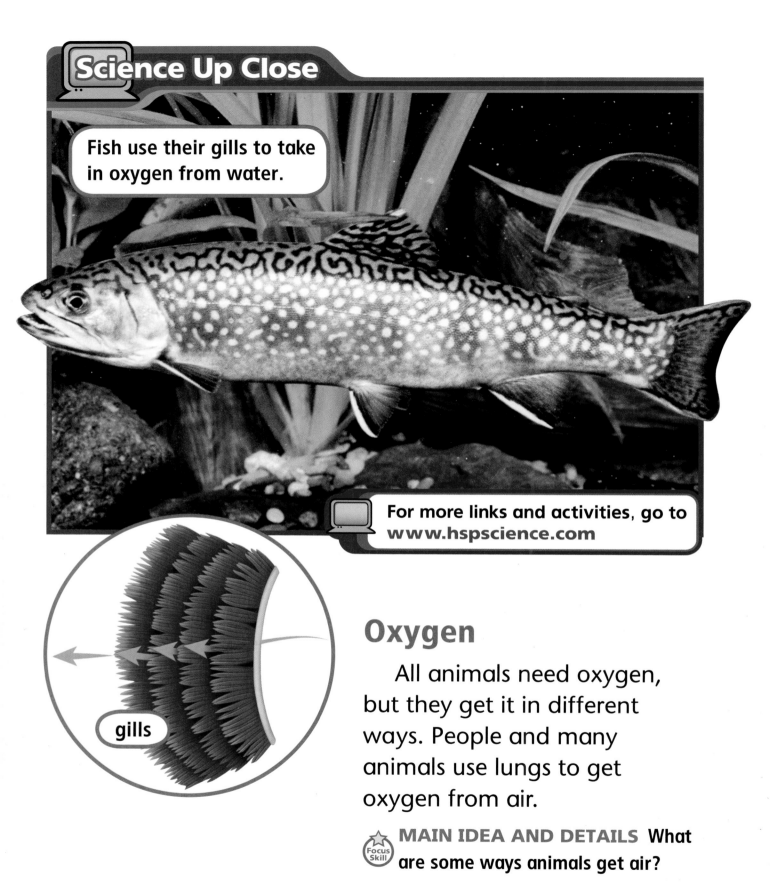

Fish use their gills to take in oxygen from water.

For more links and activities, go to www.hspscience.com

gills

Oxygen

All animals need oxygen, but they get it in different ways. People and many animals use lungs to get oxygen from air.

MAIN IDEA AND DETAILS What are some ways animals get air?

People and Environments

People can change environments. They may cut down trees and clear away other plants to build houses. When they do this, animals can lose their habitats.

Environments also change when people bring in new plants or animals. People brought water hyacinths to Florida.

The water hyacinths grew quickly and covered the water. They shut out air and light. The other plants began to die. The hyacinths used all the oxygen in the water. Then the fish died.

MAIN IDEA AND DETAILS **What can happen when people change environments?**

water hyacinths

Why Animals Have Disappeared

Some animals can not meet their needs when their environment changes. They become **extinct**, or die out.

Nature can change the environment. Dinosaurs lived on Earth millions of years ago. Then they became extinct. Scientists think that Earth became too cold for them to live.

People can also change the environment. They may cut down trees to build houses. Animals may then lose their homes and food. They may die out.

⭐ **MAIN IDEA AND DETAILS** **What can cause animals to become extinct?**

The barn owl may become extinct if people keep changing its environment. ▼

1. MAIN IDEA AND DETAILS Copy and complete this chart. Tell about environments.

Main Idea and Details

An environment is made up of living and nonliving things.

| Animals and **A** _____ live in environments. | An environment can be hot, **B** _____, **C** _____, or dry. | There are many habitats in an **D** _____. | Animals have **E** _____ for survival in an environment. |

2. DRAW CONCLUSIONS What can you tell about an animal that has thick fur?

3. VOCABULARY Use the term **adapt** to tell about this picture.

Test Prep

4. Why do some animals become extinct?

Links

Writing

Description of an Environment
Choose an animal. Describe its environment. Then draw a picture of the animal in its environment. Share your work with a classmate.

 For more links and activities, go to www.hspscience.com

How Do Living Things Survive in Different Places?

Fast Fact

Some butterflies stay safe by blending in with their environment. Making inferences will help you figure out how animals stay safe.

How Color Helps a Butterfly

You need

- **paper squares**
- **orange paper**
- **clock**

Step 1

Scatter equal numbers of purple, orange, and yellow squares on the sheet of paper. Observe the squares.

Step 2

Count the purple squares for five seconds. Record the number. Repeat for the orange and yellow squares.

Step 3

Which color squares were hardest to count? What can you **infer** about how color helps a butterfly?

Inquiry Skill

When you **infer**, you use what you see to figure out why something happened.

LS-3 Explain need for habitats; LS-6 Investigate plant/animal adaptations; SI-2 Ask "how do we know" questions; SI-6 Use observations

133

Reading in Science

LS-3 Explain need for habitats; **LS-5** Explain need for food; **LS-6** Investigate plant/animal adaptations; **LS-7** Compare Ohio habitats

VOCABULARY

desert
rain forest
grassland
tundra
ocean
pond

READING FOCUS SKILL

MAIN IDEA AND DETAILS Look for ways animals and plants have adapted to their environments.

Desert

Animals and plants have adapted to the environments they live in.

A **desert** is a dry environment that gets little rain. Few kinds of plants and animals are adapted to living there. A cactus stores water that it can use later. Lizards hide under rocks during the day, when it is hot. They come out to find food at night, when it is cool.

▲ **The veiled chameleon eats fruits, flowers, and leaves to get water.**

 MAIN IDEA AND DETAILS How have plants and animals adapted to living in deserts?

The sharp needles on a saguaro cactus keep away animals that want to eat it.

Rain Forest

A **rain forest** is a wet environment that gets rain almost every day. Many rain forests are also hot all year. They have many tall trees that block the sunlight. Some plants grow high on the trees to reach the light.

Some monkeys live high in the trees, too. They can hold onto branches with their tails. This lets them grab food with their hands. Bats hunt at night, when they can catch flying insects and other small animals.

⭐ **Focus Skill** **MAIN IDEA AND DETAILS** How have plants and animals adapted to living in rain forests?

The green tree frog has sticky feet that help it climb. ▼

135

▲ Cheetahs are the fastest animals on land. The color of gazelles helps them hide from cheetahs. The cheetahs can not see the gazelles in the grass.

Grassland

A **grassland** is an open environment that is covered with grass. Few trees grow there, so it is hard for large animals to hide. Elephants and other animals travel in groups of their own kind to stay safe. Some animals are able to run fast. This helps them stay safe.

(Focus Skill) **MAIN IDEA AND DETAILS** How have animals adapted to living in the grassland?

Keeping Warm

Does fat keep animals warm? Place shortening in a plastic bag. Put another plastic bag over each hand. Then put one hand in the bag with the shortening and the other hand in an empty bag. Put both hands in a bowl of cold water. Which hand stays warm longer?

Tundra

A **tundra** is a cold, snowy environment. Plants do not grow very tall, and they grow close together. This helps protect them from the very cold temperatures. Many tundra animals have thick fur to keep them warm. Some animals have fur that changes with the seasons. In spring, new brown fur grows in to help them hide in summer. In fall, white fur grows in to help them hide in winter.

▲ Polar bears stay warm because of their fat and their thick fur.

 MAIN IDEA AND DETAILS
How have plants and animals adapted to living in the tundra?

Caribou travel from place to place to find the plants they eat.

Ocean

An **ocean** is a large body of salt water. Most ocean plants and animals live in the top layer of the ocean. There, the plants can get the sunlight they need, and the animals can find food.

Ocean animals stay safe in many ways. Some fish change colors to help them hide. Others swim fast or hide in small cracks. A jellyfish stings other animals that come too close to it.

⭐ (Focus Skill) **MAIN IDEA AND DETAILS** How do ocean animals stay safe?

Fish have scales to protect their bodies.

A shark's sharp teeth help it catch food. Its scales and body shape help it swim quickly.

An octopus uses its eight long arms to catch food.

139

Pond

A **pond** is a small freshwater environment. Water lilies may grow on the surface of a pond. There, they can get the sunlight they need. Many animals, such as beavers, live in ponds. Beavers have webbed feet to help them swim. They use their sharp teeth to cut down trees to build their homes.

 MAIN IDEA AND DETAILS How have plants and animals adapted to living in ponds?

Water striders can walk on the surface of the pond without sinking.

water lilies

1. MAIN IDEA AND DETAILS Copy and complete this chart. Tell how plants and animals have adapted to living in their environments.

Main Idea and Details

Plants and animals have adapted to living in many environments.

| A cactus in the desert can store water. | Grassland animals travel **A** _____. | Animals that live in a tundra have thick **B** _____. | Some ocean animals change colors to **C** _____. | Plants in a pond grow where they can get **D** _____. |

2. DRAW CONCLUSIONS Why would it be hard for a rain-forest animal to live in a grassland environment?

3. VOCABULARY Use the terms **desert** and **tundra** to tell about environments.

Test Prep

4. What kind of environment does an animal with webbed feet probably live in?
   A. cold
   B. warm
   C. dry
   D. wet

Links

Math

Solve a Problem
Use this chart to find out how much more rain falls in a rain forest than in a desert. How could you solve the problem without measuring the difference? Write a math sentence that shows how.

Average Rainfall in One Month	
desert	2 cm
rain forest	20 cm

For more links and activities, go to **www.hspscience.com**

LS-1 Explore organisms' basic needs; LS-2 Identify environments; LS-3 Explain needs for habitats; LS-6 Investigate plant/animal adaptations; ST-2 Investigate how technology meets needs; SK-3 Describe effects of science on people and the environment

Helping Hawai'i's Reefs

In Hawai`i, coral reefs surround the islands. The reefs have been damaged by people and ships.

But there is help for the reefs. The United States government has passed laws to help protect the reefs around Hawai`i.

What Are Coral Reefs?

A coral reef is made up of the skeletons of tiny sea animals. A reef is often found in warm, shallow waters. More than half the United States' coral reefs are located in the waters around Hawai`i.

Coral reefs provide homes for other sea animals. Reefs also protect coastlines from dangerous waves. When waves pass over reefs, they slow down and get smaller.

How Are Reefs Formed?

A coral reef is built by tiny sea creatures called coral polyps. When coral polyps die, their hard outer skeletons stay and other polyps grow on top of the skeletons. After a long time, the coral skeletons build up, forming a reef.

A reef can also be formed by people. For example, people have made several reefs by sinking ships or even subway cars. These reefs then provide shelter for fish and a place for underwater plants to grow.

Think About It

How do coral reefs help fish to survive?

Find out more! Log on to
www.hspscience.com

SCIENCE Spin from WEEKLY READER

People

LS-1 Explore organisms' basic needs; LS-2 Identify environments; LS-3 Explain needs for habitats; LS-5 Explain need for food; LS-6 Investigate plant/ animal adaptations

PAL TO THE PANDA

Lu Zhi is a wildlife biologist. A wildlife biologist is a scientist who studies wild animals. Lu works to protect pandas.

Lu has studied giant pandas in China for most of her life. She was one of the first scientists to go into a den with a wild panda. A den is a panda's home. Panda dens are usually in a cave made of rock or in the bottom of a hollow tree.

Pandas live in forest areas where a plant called bamboo is found. Bamboo is a type of grass that pandas eat. Lu works to protect these forest areas.

SCIENCE Projects
for Home or School
You Can Do It!

What Seeds Need

You need
- bean seeds
- 2 zip-top bags
- wet paper towel
- dry paper towel

What to Do

1. Put a few seeds and a very wet paper towel in a bag. Close the bag.
2. Put a few seeds and a dry paper towel in a bag. Close the bag tightly.
3. Observe the seeds each day for a week.

Draw Conclusions

What happened to the seeds in each bag? What things do seeds need to grow?

Worm World

Fill a large jar with wet soil. Place earthworms on the soil. Sprinkle soil and leaves over the earthworms. How does the environment help the worms get what they need to live?

LS-1 Explore organisms' basic needs; **LS-2** Identify environments; **LS-3** Explain need for habitats; **LS-5** Explain need for food; **SI-6** Use observations

145

Review and Test Preparation

Vocabulary Review

Use the terms below to complete the sentences. The page numbers tell you where to look if you need help.

oxygen p. 108   **environment** p. 124
survive p. 108   **adapt** p. 126
shelter p. 111   **extinct** p. 130

1. Living things need food, water, and oxygen to _____.

2. When an animal dies out, it becomes _____.

3. A gas that all living things need is _____.

4. All the living and nonliving things in a place make up an _____.

5. A safe place to live is called a _____.

6. When animals change over time to be able to live in their environment, they _____.

Check Understanding

7. Compare these dogs. How are they alike? How are they different?

8. Compare these plants. What do they both need to survive?

Critical Thinking

These pictures show what an arctic fox looks like in winter and in summer.

9. Tell how the fox has adapted to living in its environment.

10. What might happen to an animal if people introduce a new animal into its environment?

4 Living Things Need Energy

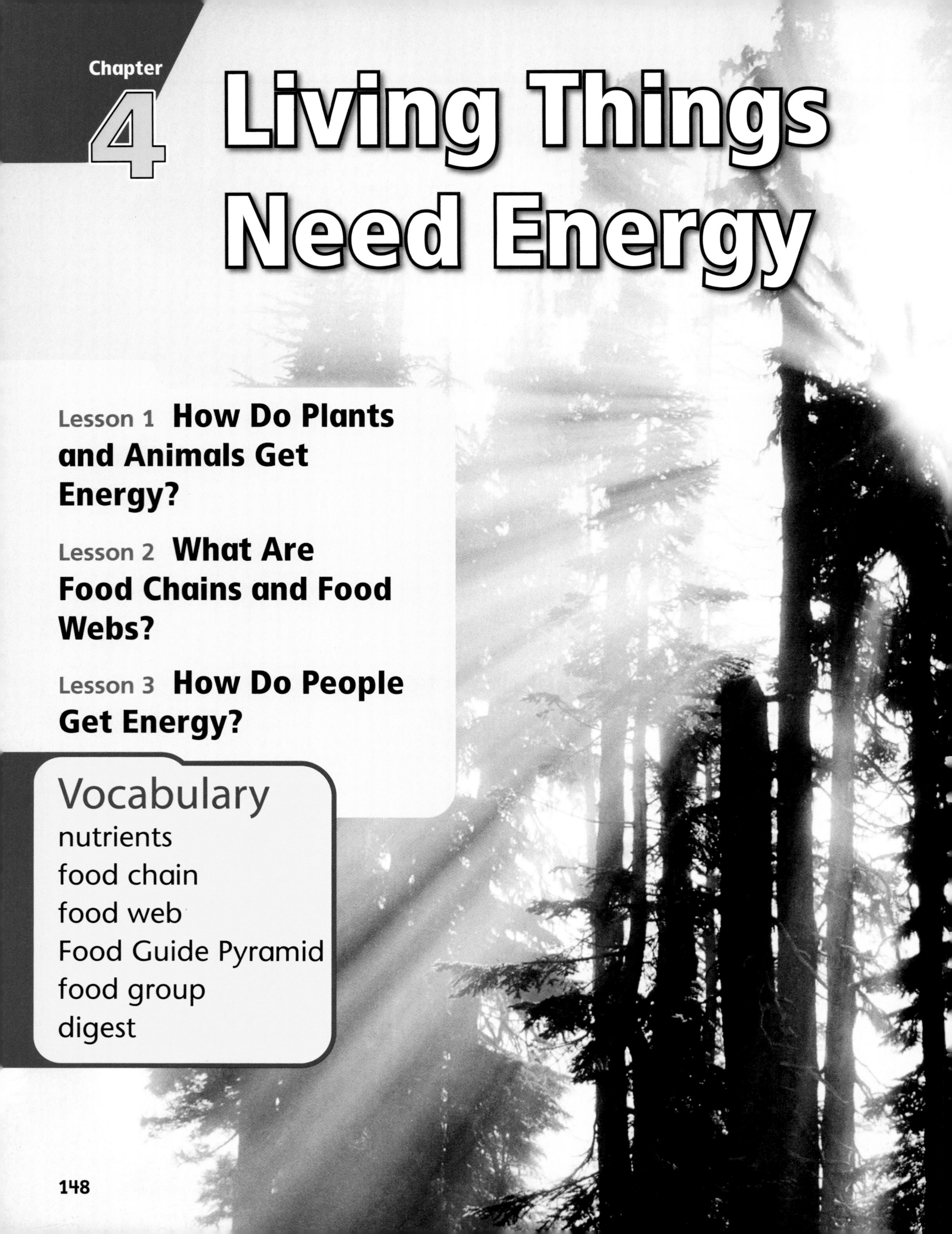

Lesson 1 How Do Plants and Animals Get Energy?

Lesson 2 What Are Food Chains and Food Webs?

Lesson 3 How Do People Get Energy?

Vocabulary

nutrients
food chain
food web
Food Guide Pyramid
food group
digest

I wonder...

Why do trees need the sun?

What do you wonder?

149

How Do Plants and Animals Get Energy?

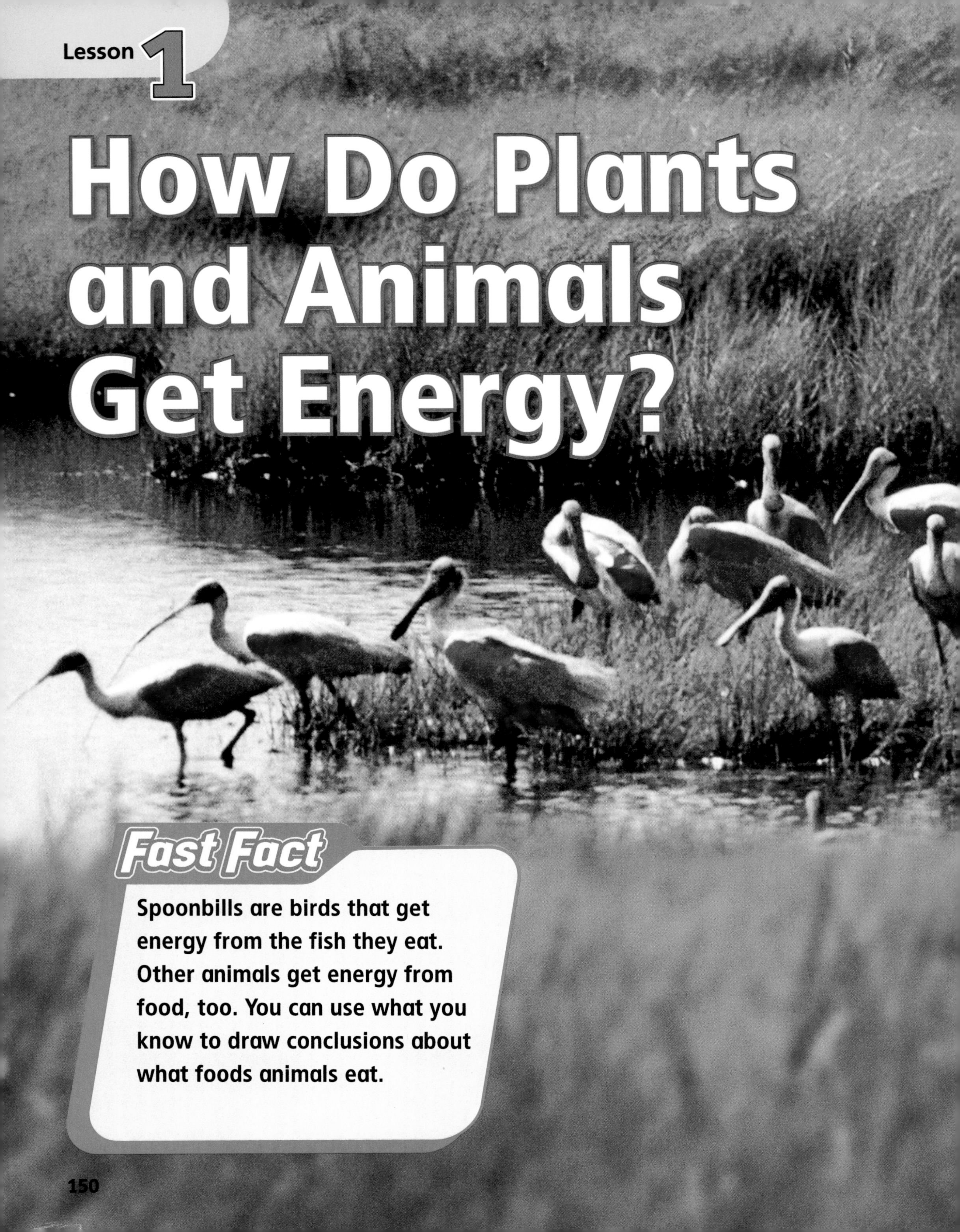

Fast Fact

Spoonbills are birds that get energy from the fish they eat. Other animals get energy from food, too. You can use what you know to draw conclusions about what foods animals eat.

How Plants Get Energy

You need

- **2 plants**

- **foil**

Step 1

Cover the leaves of one plant with foil.

Step 2

Put both plants in a place that gets a lot of light. Water them both when the soil is dry. Wait one week.

Step 3

Remove the foil. Observe and compare the plants. **Draw conclusions** about which plant got the energy it needed and why.

Inquiry Skill

Use your observations and what you know to **draw conclusions**.

LS-1 Explore organisms' basic needs; **LS-5** Explain need for food; **LS-6** Investigate plant/ animal adaptations; **SI-6** Use observations

151

VOCABULARY
nutrients

 READING FOCUS SKILL

MAIN IDEA AND DETAILS
Look for details about the ways plants
and animals get energy.

Plants

All living things need energy to
live. They get energy from food.

Plants make their own food.
They use energy from sunlight to
make the food. Plants also use air,
water, and **nutrients**. Nutrients are
substances that plants and animals
need to grow and stay healthy.

▲ This plant is growing
toward the sunlight.

Water lilies have leaves that
float on the top of the water,
where they can get sunlight.

Plants grow where they can get all the things they need to make food. Different parts of a plant help it get air, sunlight, and water. Leaves take in air and the energy in sunlight. Roots take in water and nutrients from the soil.

 MAIN IDEA AND DETAILS What do plants need to make food?

Soil and Water

Place a rock and a small amount of soil on a plate. Pour a little water on top of each. What happens to the water? How do plants use soil to get water?

Roots take in nutrients and water the plants need to make food. ▼

153

Animals

Animals need energy to live, just as plants do. Like plants, animals get energy from food. Unlike plants, animals can not make their own food.

Animals catch or find food where they live. Some animals eat plants. Some eat other animals. Some eat both plants and animals.

 MAIN IDEA AND DETAILS How do animals get energy?

▲ A caterpillar gets energy from leaves.

▼ A puffin gets energy from fish.

A panda gets energy from bamboo.

1. MAIN IDEA AND DETAILS Copy and complete this chart. Tell how plants and animals get energy.

Main Idea and Details

Plants and animals get energy from food.

| Plants **A** _____ their own food. | Plants need sunlight, air, **B** _____, and **C** _____. | Animals catch or **D** _____ food. | Animals eat **E** _____ or other animals to get energy. |

2. SUMMARIZE Use the chart to write a lesson summary.

3. VOCABULARY Use the term **nutrients** to tell about this picture.

Test Prep

4. Why do animals eat plants and other animals?

Links

Writing

Chart of What Animals Eat
Make a chart that lists three animals. Do research to find out whether they eat plants, animals, or both. Then fill in your chart. Compare it with the charts your classmates made.

What Animals Eat		
animal	what it eats	
	animals	plants
eagle		
horse		
rabbit		

For more links and activities, go to www.hspscience.com

What Are Food Chains and Food Webs?

Fast Fact

This blue heron eats fish. You can communicate what you learn about what animals eat.

What Animals Eat

You need

 • animal cards    • books about animals    • markers

Step 1

Choose a picture of an animal. Find out what that animal eats.

Step 2

Draw and label a picture of the food.

Step 3

Use your pictures and cards to **communicate** your ideas.

Inquiry Skill

When you **communicate** your ideas, you tell what you know.

LS-1 Explore organisms' basic needs; **LS-5** Explain need for food; **SI-10** Communicate observations

157

VOCABULARY

food chain
food web

 READING FOCUS SKILL

SEQUENCE Look for the order in which animals eat other living things.

Food Chains

Living things need one another to survive. A **food chain** shows the order in which animals eat plants and other animals.

Food chains start with sunlight and plants. In this food chain, first, the grass uses sunlight to make its food. Second, a grasshopper eats the grass. Third, a frog eats the grasshopper. Fourth, a snake eats the frog. Last, a hawk eats the snake.

 SEQUENCE What happens after a grasshopper eats grass?

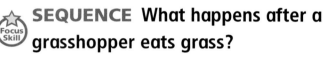

Insta-Lab

Food Chain Mix-Up

On three index cards, draw a plant and two animals that all belong in the same food chain. Mix up the cards, and ask a partner to put them in the right order. Have your partner explain how the food chain works.

Food Webs

Most animals eat more than one kind of food. So an animal may be part of more than one food chain. Connected food chains make up a **food web**. Look at this food web. Use the arrows to find out the foods each animal eats.

 SEQUENCE What happens after the rabbit eats the grass?

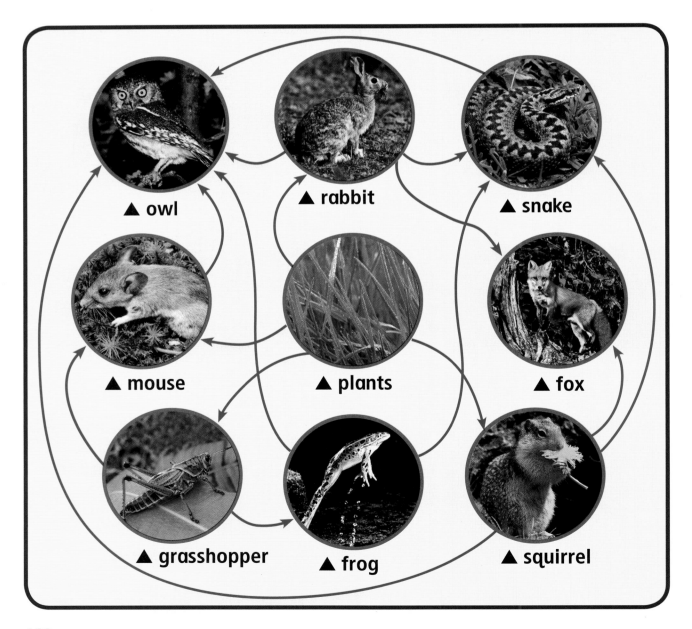

▲ owl

▲ rabbit

▲ snake

▲ mouse

▲ plants

▲ fox

▲ grasshopper

▲ frog

▲ squirrel

1. SEQUENCE Copy and complete this chart to show a food chain.

Food Chain

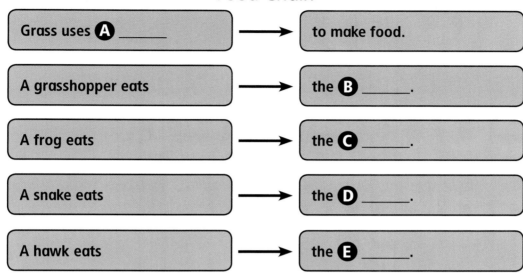

Grass uses **A** _____	→	to make food.
A grasshopper eats	→	the **B** _____.
A frog eats	→	the **C** _____.
A snake eats	→	the **D** _____.
A hawk eats	→	the **E** _____.

2. SUMMARIZE Write two sentences that tell what this lesson is about.

3. VOCABULARY Explain the difference between a **food chain** and a **food web**.

Test Prep

4. Which is a food chain?
  A. plants, fox, mouse
  B. plants, squirrel, fox
  C. snake, plants, frog
  D. grasshopper, frog, plants

Links

Art

Food Web Mobile

On index cards, draw and label plants and animals that make up a food web. Punch a hole in the top, the bottom, and both sides of each card. Connect the cards with yarn to show how the food web works. Then hang the cards from a hanger.

 For more links and activities, go to **www.hspscience.com**

How Do People Get Energy?

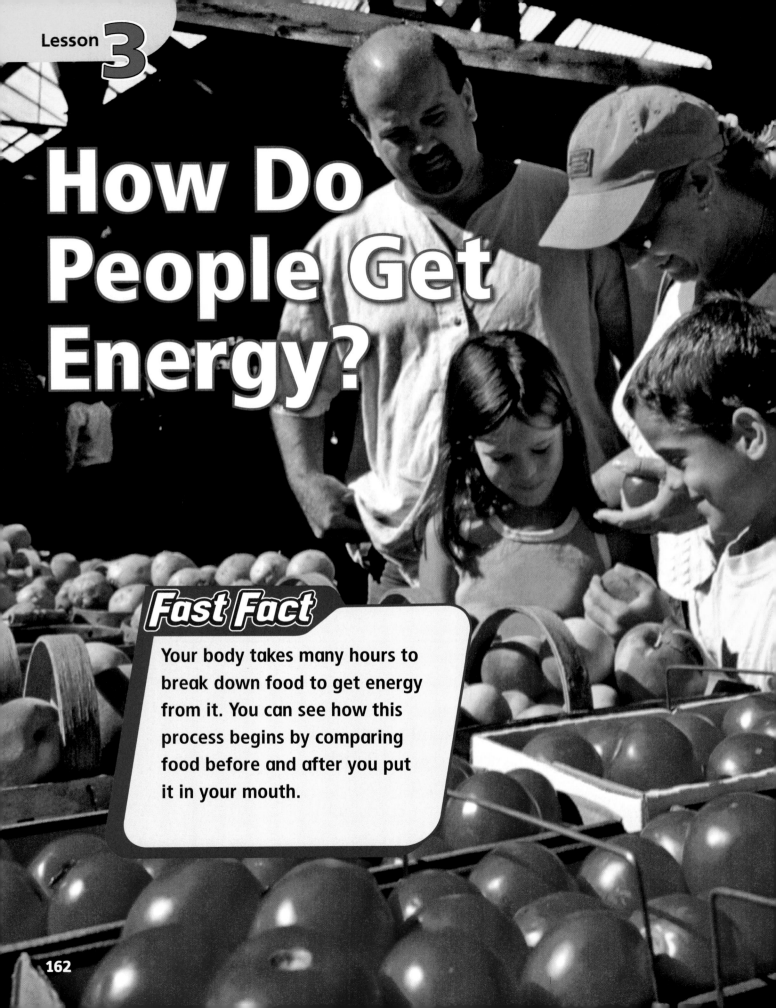

Fast Fact

Your body takes many hours to break down food to get energy from it. You can see how this process begins by comparing food before and after you put it in your mouth.

How People Get Energy

You need

- cracker

- mirror

Step 1

Observe a cracker. Draw it. Put a small piece of cracker in your mouth. Do not chew it.

Step 2

Count slowly to 20. Open your mouth, and use the mirror to observe the cracker. Draw what you observe.

Step 3

Compare your pictures. Tell what you think made the cracker change.

Inquiry Skill

You can see how something changes when you compare the way it was before to the way it is after.

LS-1 Explore organisms' basic needs; **LS-5** Explain need for food

VOCABULARY
Food Guide
  Pyramid
food group
digest

 READING FOCUS SKILL

CAUSE AND EFFECT Look for the effects eating food has on your body.

Energy from Food

Like all living things, you need water, air, and food to live. You need water to drink. You need air to breathe. You need food to eat. Your body gets the energy it needs from the food you eat.

The children are getting energy from the watermelon. ▼

The food you eat gives you energy to do all the things you do each day. Your body uses energy when you walk, run, ride a bike, swim, and play. It even uses energy when you read, speak, and think.

CAUSE AND EFFECT What happens when you walk or speak?

Insta-Lab

Using Energy

Your body uses energy even when you do not move. Sit very still for 30 seconds. Observe ways your body is using energy. Talk with a partner about the things you both observed.

Food Guide Pyramid

You need to eat different kinds of foods to stay healthy. The **Food Guide Pyramid** helps you choose what to eat and how much of it to eat. It also shows which food group each food belongs to. A **food group** is a group of foods that provide most of the same kinds of nutrient.

The foods in each food group help your body in a different way. Milk, yogurt, and cheese help keep your teeth and bones strong. Meat, fish, eggs, and nuts help build your body. Whole grains, fresh fruits, and vegetables are foods that contain sugar. They give your body most of its energy.

 CAUSE AND EFFECT What happens when you eat foods from different food groups?

milk, yogurt, and cheese

vegetables

fats, oils, and sweets

meat, poultry, fish, dried beans, eggs, and nuts

fruits

breads, cereals, rice, and pasta

Digesting Foods

Your body must **digest**, or break down, food to get energy and nutrients from it.

Your teeth and saliva break up and soften food in your mouth. Your stomach muscles squeeze the food and mix it with special juices. The food becomes a thick liquid.

As the food moves through your intestines, your blood takes nutrients from it. The blood then carries the nutrients to all the other parts of your body. The food parts your body does not need move out of your body as waste.

☆ **CAUSE AND EFFECT** What causes solid food to become a liquid?

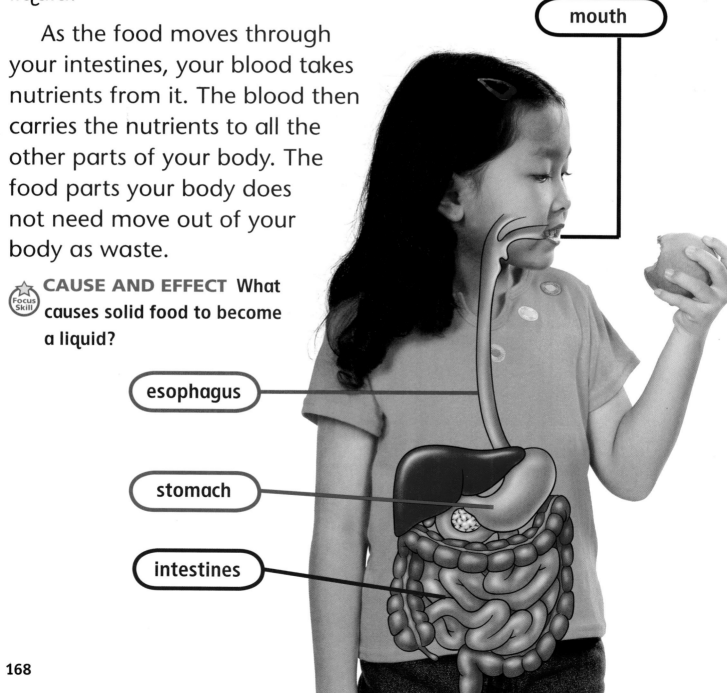

mouth

esophagus

stomach

intestines

1. CAUSE AND EFFECT Copy and complete this chart. Tell the effect of each cause.

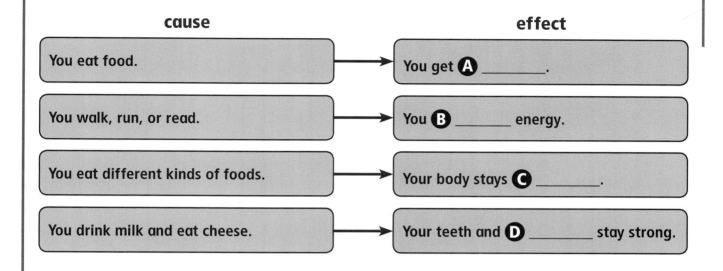

cause	effect
You eat food.	You get **A** _____.
You walk, run, or read.	You **B** _____ energy.
You eat different kinds of foods.	Your body stays **C** _____.
You drink milk and eat cheese.	Your teeth and **D** _____ stay strong.

2. SUMMARIZE Write a summary of this lesson. Begin with the sentence **People need food to get energy.**

3. VOCABULARY Use the term **digest** to tell about this picture.

Test Prep
4. How do people get energy?

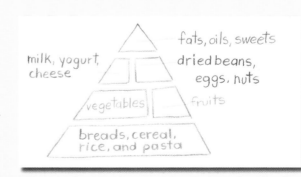

Links

Health

Classify What You Eat
List everything you ate for lunch today or yesterday. Then draw and label the Food Guide Pyramid. Write each food from your list in the correct food group.

fats, oils, sweets
milk, yogurt, cheese
dried beans, eggs, nuts
vegetables
fruits
breads, cereal, rice, and pasta

For more links and activities, go to www.hspscience.com

DIETS FOR ATHLETES

An athlete who competes in the Olympics must train very hard. But all that training takes a lot of energy. What do athletes do to help them train better? They eat, of course!

One young Olympic athlete in training ate the same thing almost every day. He ate two bowls of cereal, two fried-egg-and-cheese sandwiches, three slices of French toast, grits, chocolate-chip pancakes, shrimp, salad, steak, sweet potatoes, broccoli with cheese, and ice cream or a brownie sundae.

Of course, only top athletes in training should eat that much. Most people should eat a lot less. And they should also choose the right kinds of foods to eat.

Think About It

Where do you get your energy from?

A CASE OF ATHLETE'S FOOD

Athletes must eat a lot of food to keep up their energy and strength. They must eat different kinds of foods. The foods they usually eat the most are breads, cereals, pasta, and potatoes.

Find out more! Log on to
www.hspscience.com

We All Need Energy

Marcus Johnson was excited to meet Penelope. Penelope is a snake who lives at a library in Greenville, South Carolina. During a visit to the library, Marcus learned a lot about snakes and about Penelope.

Penelope is a python. Pythons are large, nonvenomous snakes. They can grow to be 10 meters (33 feet) long! A snake that big needs lots of energy. While visiting Penelope, Marcus learned what pythons eat to get their energy.

Pythons are part of a food chain. They eat mostly small animals such as mice and birds. Pythons get their prey, or food, by squeezing it.

LS-1 Explore organisms' basic needs; LS-5 Explain need for food

You Can Do It!

How the Stomach Works

What to Do

1. Put crushed crackers and water in the bag. Seal it.

2. The bag is a model of your stomach. Slowly squeeze the bag to show what your stomach muscles do to food.

3. Observe what happens.

Materials

- small zip-top bag
- crackers
- water

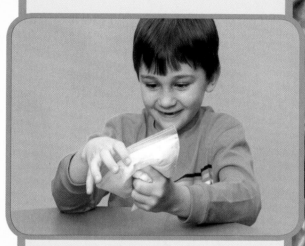

Draw Conclusions

What happens to food in your stomach? How does the stomach help your body digest foods?

How Much Energy Is in Food?

You can find out how much energy is in food by looking at labels on food packages. Energy is measured in calories. Make a chart to show how many calories are in one serving of some different foods. List the foods in order from most to fewest calories.

Energy in Food

food	calories in 1 serving
raisins	130
bread	120
orange juice	110
milk	100
cheese	70
green beans	20

LS-1 Explore organisms' basic needs; **LS-5** Explain need for food; **SI-6** Use observations; **SI-9** Use numbers

173

Review and Test Preparation

Vocabulary Review

Use the terms below to complete the sentences. The page numbers tell you where to look if you need help.

nutrients p. 152   **food web** p. 160

food chain p. 158   **food group** p. 166

1. A group of foods of the same kind is a _____.

2. A _____ shows the order in which animals eat plants and other animals.

3. Food chains that are connected make up a _____.

4. Minerals that plants and animals need are _____.

Check Understanding

5. Write **first, next, then,** and **last** to
show the sequence in this food chain.

_____   _____   _____   _____

6. What is always at the beginning of a
food chain?

A. fish

B. light and plants

C. owls

D. trees and birds

Critical Thinking

7. What can happen to a food web if a
new animal is added to an environment?

8. What would happen to people or
animals that did not eat the food
they needed?

5 Living Things in Ohio

Lesson 1 How Do Seasons Change Plants?

Lesson 2 How Do Seasons Change Animals?

Lesson 3 What Are Some Ohio Habitats?

Vocabulary

season	forest
nectar	grassland
camouflage	prairie
forage	wetland
migrate	
hibernate	
habitat	

I wonder...

How will this fox stay warm in winter?

What do you wonder?

How Do Seasons Change Plants?

Fast Fact

The marsh marigold is one of the
first plants to bloom each spring
in Ohio. You can communicate
what you observe about how
plants change.

Life Cycle of a Bean Plant

You need

- cup filled with soil
- pencil
- beans
- water

Step 1

Use the pencil to make holes in the soil. Put a bean in each hole. Cover the beans with soil. Wash your hands when you finish.

Step 2

Water the soil. Put the cup in a warm, sunny place.

Step 3

Observe the cup each day for two weeks. Water the soil when it is dry. Draw what you observe. **Communicate** what is happening.

Inquiry Skill

You can use pictures to help you **communicate**.

LS-1 Explore organisms' basic needs; LS-5 Explain need for food; SI-4 Use safety precautions; SI-6 Use observations; SI-10 Communicate explanations

179

Reading in Science

LS-1 Explore organisms' basic needs; **LS-2** Identify environments; **LS-4** Compare organisms; **LS-5** Explain need for food; **LS-7** Compare Ohio habitats; **LS-9** Compare Ohio plants

VOCABULARY
season
nectar

READING FOCUS SKILL

SEQUENCE Look for the order in which plants change each season.

How Trees Change

A **season** is a time of year with a certain kind of weather. Plants, such as the Ohio Buckeye tree, change when the seasons change.

In spring, the Ohio Buckeye is one of the first trees in Ohio to get new leaves. Soon flowers bloom on the branches. The **nectar**, or sugary liquid in the flowers, attract birds, butterflies, and bees.

During summer, fruit grows on the tree and gets ripe. It falls to the ground.

spring

summer

▲ buckeye flower

fall

▲ A buckeye seed grows in each fruit.

winter

In fall, the tree changes again. The leaves change color from green to bright orange and yellow. Then they drop off. The Ohio Buckeye is one of the first trees in Ohio to lose its leaves every fall.

During the hard winter, the large branches of the Ohio Buckeye do not break under the heavy snow. The branches have no leaves. They will not grow back again until spring. Then the cycle will begin again.

 SEQUENCE How does the Ohio Buckeye change from spring to winter?

How a Tree Changes
Look out the window. Draw a picture of a tree you see. Write the season below the picture. Then draw a picture of what the tree will look like in a different season.

How Crops Change

Like all plants, crop plants change each season. Tomatoes are crop plants.

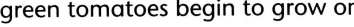

A tomato seed begins to grow when it gets warmth, air, and water. First, the root grows down. The root takes in nutrients and water from the soil. The root also helps hold the plant in place. Next, the stem of the tiny plant breaks through the ground.

During spring, the stem grows into vines. Leaves and yellow flowers grow on the vines. The leaves make food for the plant. At the end of spring or early summer, green tomatoes begin to grow on the stems.

▲ Pumpkins are a crop that changes each season. A pumpkin changes from green to orange in late summer and early fall.

During summer, the green tomatoes get bigger. They change color and become red. They also get softer. In late summer and early fall, the tomatoes are ripe. They are ready to be picked.

The plant dies in winter when the weather gets cold. The cycle begins again when new plants start to grow in spring.

SEQUENCE What happens to a tomato plant after spring?

Wildflowers

More than 2,300 kinds of wildflowers grow in Ohio. You can see them in different places. They grow in fields and in woods. Some wildflowers grow in dry soil. Others grow near wet places, such as swamps, lakes, and streams.

Many wildflowers bloom in spring. They have colors of blue, pink, yellow, white, and red. Different wildflowers bloom in spring and fall.

 **SEQUENCE** What happens to wildflowers in spring?

▲ **The swamp buttercup grows in wet places. It has yellow flowers.**

▼ **The large-flowered trillium grows in the woods. It has flowers that change from white to pink.**

1. SEQUENCE Copy and complete the chart. Tell, in order, how a tree changes during each season.

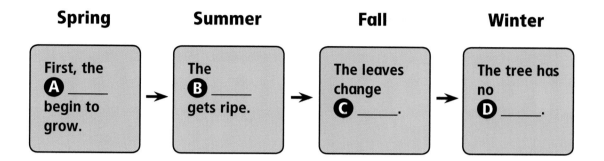

Spring	Summer	Fall	Winter
First, the **A**____ begin to grow.	The **B**____ gets ripe.	The leaves change **C**____.	The tree has no **D**____.

2. DRAW CONCLUSIONS Why do some plants die in winter?

3. VOCABULARY How do the **seasons** affect plants?

Test Prep

4. Where do wildflowers grow?

Links

Writing

Description of Changes
Choose a kind of plant. Pretend you are that plant. Describe the changes that happen to you each season. Draw pictures to show what you wrote about.

Leaves are starting to grow on my branches.

 For more links and activities, go to www.hspscience.com

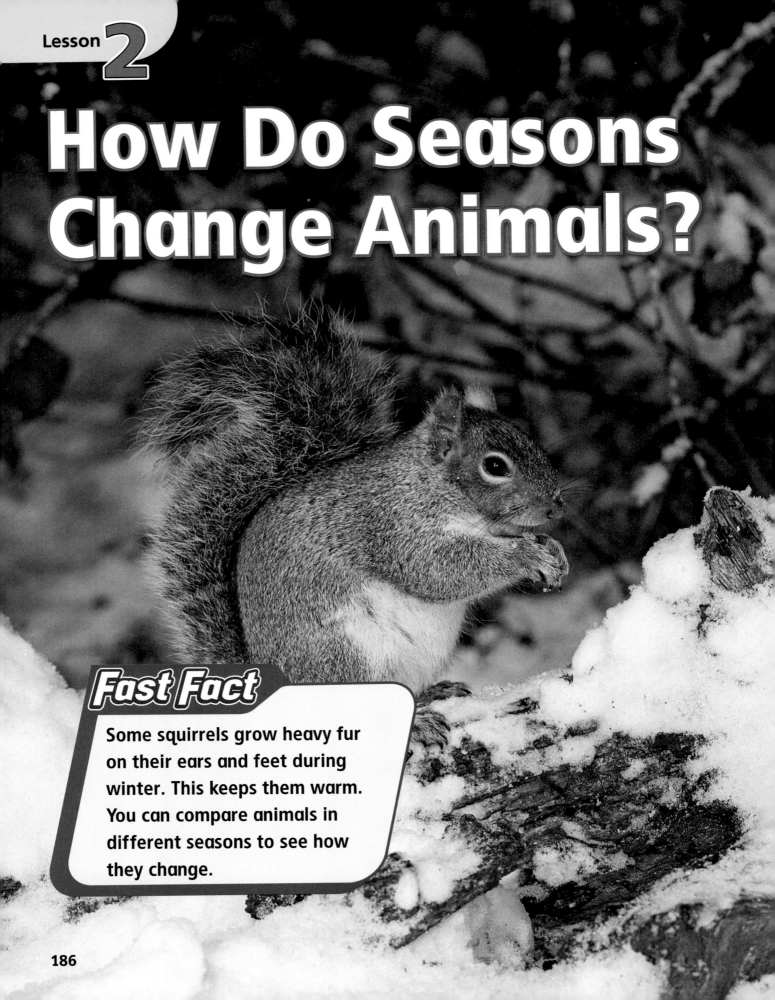

How Do Seasons Change Animals?

Fast Fact

Some squirrels grow heavy fur on their ears and feet during winter. This keeps them warm. You can compare animals in different seasons to see how they change.

Compare Hair and Feathers

You need

• feather

• hand lens

Step 1

Observe the feather with the hand lens. What does it look like and feel like?

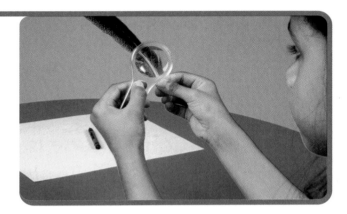

Step 2

Observe the hair on your arm. **Compare** the hair with the feather.

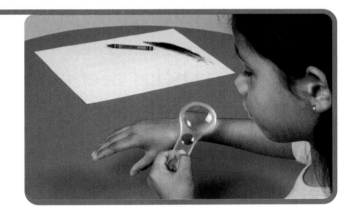

Step 3

Draw pictures of what you observed. Write about how the feather and hair are alike and different.

Inquiry Skill

Comparing hair and a feather helps you understand how kinds of animals are alike and different.

LS-6 Investigate plant/animal adaptations; **SI-6** Use observations; **SI-7** Use scientific equipment and tools **187**

Reading in Science

LS-1 Explore organisms' basic needs; LS-2 Identify environments; LS-5 Explain need for food; LS-6 Investigate plant/animal adaptations; LS-7 Compare Ohio habitats; LS-8 Compare Ohio animal activities; SI-9 Use numbers

VOCABULARY

camouflage
forage
migrate
hibernate

READING FOCUS SKILL

MAIN IDEA AND DETAILS Look for the ways animals change in different seasons.

Staying Safe

Many animals change when the seasons change. These changes help them survive in different seasons.

Some animals change by using camouflage. **Camouflage** is a way an animal looks that helps it hide. Deer have fur that changes colors. In summer, their fur is tan or red-brown. In winter, their fur is gray-brown. The color change helps deer hide in their environment. This helps them stay safe.

▲ white-tail deer in summer

MAIN IDEA AND DETAILS Why do some animals change colors with the seasons?

white-tail deer in winter ▶

Getting Food

When seasons change, some animals can not find food where they live. They must **forage**, or search for food. They may also eat different foods in winter when they can not find the foods they like in summer.

Other animals, such as squirrels, chipmunks, and beavers, gather and store food in the fall. Then the animals eat it in winter when food is hard to find.

▲ Chipmunks collect seeds in fall to eat in winter.

MAIN IDEA AND DETAILS Why do some animals move to different places?

The Life Cycle of a Frog

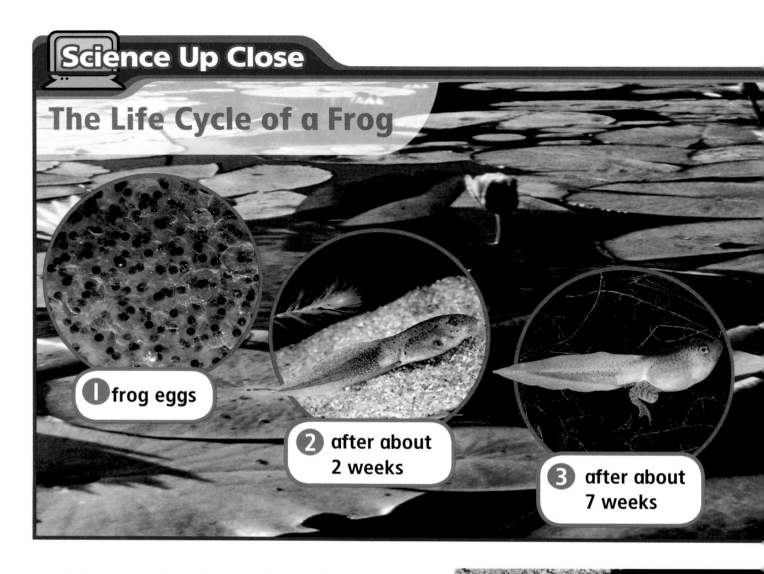

1 frog eggs

2 after about 2 weeks

3 after about 7 weeks

Many animals, such as frogs, have their young in spring. Frog mothers lay their eggs. A tadpole, or young frog, hatches from an egg. A tadpole lives in a pond or other body of water. It uses its tail to swim.

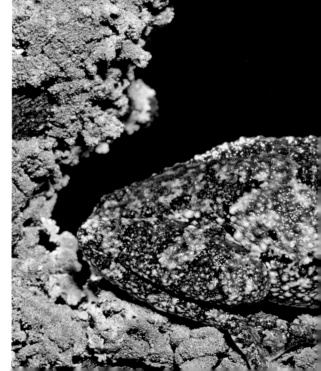

5 after about 14 weeks

4 after about 9 weeks

For more links and activities, go to
www.hspscience.com

Next, the tadpole gets bigger and grows two back legs. Then, the tadpole starts to look more like a frog. It still has a tail, and now it has four legs.

Last, the frog is fully grown and has no tail. It lives on land most of the time. Some frogs can change their colors to hide.

⭐ **MAIN IDEA AND DETAILS** How is a tadpole different from a frog?

Staying Warm

In winter, animals need to stay warm. Some animals, such as the red fox, grow more fur. This extra body covering helps keep them warm. In summer, they lose the extra fur.

Other animals stay close together. Some snakes live together in holes. Bees cluster together. This keeps them warm.

▲ red fox

▼ Bees cluster in a ball during winter to stay warm. They eat the honey they made in summer.

▲ The monarch butterfly migrates from Ohio each fall. It lives in Mexico during the winter.

Winter is too cold for some animals. It is also hard for them to find food. So these animals migrate in fall. **Migrate** means to move and live in another place.

Butterflies, some bats, and many birds migrate in fall to find food in warmer places. In spring they return.

MAIN IDEA AND DETAILS How do different animals stay warm?

▲ Each fall, robins fly south and return to the north in spring.

Sleeping

Some animals **hibernate**, or spend the winter in a deep sleep. Their breathing and heartbeat slow. Their body temperature falls.

When animals hibernate, they do not need to eat. This helps them get through winter, when there is little food. Animals such as some bats and squirrels hibernate.

Some animals, such as black bears, do not hibernate in winter, yet they are still not active. Their bodies slow down. But their temperature falls only a little.

 MAIN IDEA AND DETAILS
How do animals change when they hibernate?

Sleeping and Breathing
Count how many breaths you take in 15 seconds. Then run in place for 30 seconds. Now how many breaths do you take in 15 seconds? Why do you think animals breathe slower when they sleep?

Focus Skill

1. **MAIN IDEA AND DETAILS** Copy and complete this chart. Tell details about animals and seasons.

Animals Change When Seasons Change.

| The color of a deer's **A**_____ changes in winter. | Birds **B**_____ in the fall. They return in spring. | A red fox grows more fur in **C**_____. | Some animals gather **D**_____ in fall to eat in winter. |

2. SUMMARIZE Write a summary of the lesson. Begin with the sentence **Many animals change with the seasons.**

3. VOCABULARY Use the term **migrate** to tell about some birds and other animals.

Test Prep

4. Why do some animals hibernate?

Links

Math

Count Heartbeats

A woodchuck's heart usually beats 80 times a minute. When it hibernates, it beats only 5 times a minute. Write a math sentence to find out how many fewer times a woodchuck's heart beats in a minute when it is hibernating.

 For more links and activities, go to **www.hspscience.com**

Lesson **3**

What Are Some Ohio Habitats?

Fast Fact

Many birds rest in Ohio's marshlands during their migrations in the fall and spring. When you observe habitats, you can learn about the animals and plants that live in them.

196

What Birds Eat

You need

- dish of birdseed
- dish of berries
- dish of breadcrumbs

Step 1

With your teacher, place three kinds of bird food outside where birds can find them.

Step 2

Observe the food in the morning, at noon, and in the afternoon. Record your **observations** in a chart.

What Birds Eat			
	birdseed	berries	bread crumbs
morning			
noon			
afternoon			

Step 3

Use your chart to share with others your findings about what the birds near your school like to eat.

Inquiry Skill

Observing animals can help you understand the kinds of food they like to eat.

Reading in Science

VOCABULARY

habitat
forest
grassland
prairie
wetland

(Focus Skill) READING FOCUS SKILL

COMPARE AND CONTRAST Look for ways habitats are alike and different.

Forests

Ohio has many habitats. A **habitat** is a place where living things have the food, water, and shelter they need. Ohio has forests, prairies, wetlands, and water habitats.

A **forest** is a habitat that gets enough rain and warmth for many trees to grow. When the weather turns cold, many of the trees lose their leaves.

cardinal

Animals use trees and other plants in a forest for food and shelter. A raccoon may live in a tree hole. Birds eat seeds and fruit. Many birds use parts of plants to build nests.

Animals help plants by moving their seeds to new growing places. Birds and bats eat seeds. Then, the animals fly to other places. Later, the seeds fall to the ground in the animals' droppings. The seeds may grow into new plants far from the plant they came from.

COMPARE AND CONTRAST What do animals and plants need in a habitat?

Squirrels bury seeds that they will eat later. Some of the seeds grow into trees. ▶

Grasslands

A **grassland** is a habitat that is covered with grass. Few trees grow there.

A **prairie** is a kind of grassland. A prairie has plants that do not grow in most other habitats. Tall grass and wildflowers grow on the Ohio prairies. The grass is green in spring and summer. In fall, the grass changes to a golden yellow.

▲ wildflowers

Big bluestem grass grows on most Ohio prairies. It can grow to more than six feet tall.

Prairie animals and plants depend on each other. Bees help flowers make seeds. The flower makes nectar. It is food for the bee.

A prairie has few trees for animals to use as homes. So, many animals, such as snakes and badgers, make homes below ground. Foxes use dens for shelter.

▲ Bees help flowers make seeds.

COMPARE AND CONTRAST How is a prairie different from a forest?

▲ Rabbits find shelter underground in holes called burrows.

▼ meadowlark and young in nest

Finding Shelter
Curl your finger in a ball of clay to make a curved hole. Sprinkle water on top. Tell how underground homes make good shelters for animals.

Wetlands

A **wetland** is a habitat that is covered by water for part of each year. In the summer, some wetlands may dry up. Swamps, marshes, and bogs are all kinds of wetlands.

Animals in a wetland need its plants to survive. Young ducks hide from owls and hawks in wetland grasses. Wetland plants take harmful things out of the water. This makes the water cleaner for animals.

▲ Many endangered animals, such as the bald eagle, depend on wetlands to survive.

 **COMPARE AND CONTRAST** How may wetlands change during the year?

▼ wetlands

yellow perch

Water

Ohio has many water habitats. Some are ponds and lakes. Others are rivers and streams.

Cattails are plants that grow in many Ohio ponds. Some animals, such as beavers, use cattails for food. Many birds nest in them.

Fish live in lakes, streams, and ponds. Some turtles also live there. They eat frogs and fish.

river turtle

 COMPARE AND CONTRAST What do turtles eat?

Ohio Habitats

These are some habitats in Ohio. Can you name which habitat each picture shows?

Focus Skill **COMPARE AND CONTRAST** How are they alike? How are they different?

1. COMPARE AND CONTRAST Draw and complete this chart. Tell how habitats are alike and different.

Habitats

alike

> Places where living things get food, **A** _____, and shelter.

different

> A forest has many **B** _____.

> A prairie has grass and **C** _____.

> A wetland is covered with **D** _____.

2. DRAW CONCLUSIONS What might happen to a forest if it did not get rain for a long time?

3. VOCABULARY Use the terms **prairie** and **grassland** to tell about a habitat in Ohio.

Test Prep

4. Which habitat is covered by water?
  A. forest
  B. grassland
  C. prairie
  D. wetland

Links

 Social Studies

Eagles in Ohio

In 1975, very few bald eagles lived in Ohio. Since then, more eagles live in Ohio. Find out more about eagles or other animals in Ohio. Share your information with the class.

 For more links and activities, go to **www.hspscience.com**

Tomato Says, "Pass the Salt!"

According to experts, a large amount of U.S. farmland is too salty. They say that each year, about 101,000 square kilometers (38,000 square miles) of U.S. farmland can not be used. The soil has too much salt.

Most plants can't grow in soil that has too much salt. But scientists have made a new kind of tomato that grows well in salty soil. The plant can even be watered with salty water.

A New Kind of Plant

Scientists have figured out a way to change how a tomato plant grows. The change allows the tomato plant to absorb salty water. The plant stores salt in its leaves, where it will not harm the plant or the fruit.

The scientists who grew the special tomatoes are also working on making other plants that can live in salty soil.

Think About It

How might plants that can grow in salty soil help farmers?

Salt of the Earth

Scientists say that plants such as corn, wheat, and peas could all be changed to be able to grow in salty soil.

Find out more! Log on to
www.hspscience.com

How Much Rain?

Brian Kessler knows plants need water. He has learned that plants get water when it rains.

Water comes from the water cycle. "I like how the water cycle works," says Brian. In the water cycle, water becomes a gas in the air, forms clouds, and comes back to Earth as rain or snow.

At home, Brian uses a weather tool. It is called a rain gauge. The rain gauge measures how much rain falls. Brian uses his rain gauge to keep track of how much rain falls at his home.

You Can Do It!

How Body Coverings Help Animals

You need
- 2 thermometers
- mitten
- record sheet
- freezer

What to Do

1. Make sure the thermometers show the same temperature. Record the temperature.

2. Put one thermometer in the mitten. Put both of the thermometers in the freezer. Wait 10 minutes.

3. Take the thermometers out of the freezer. Record the temperatures.

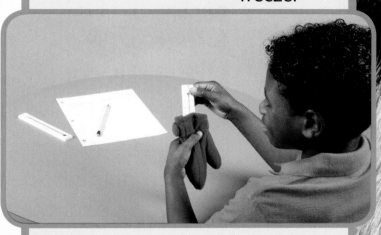

Draw Conclusions

How is the mitten like an animal's body covering? Why do you think animals grow extra fur in the winter?

Observe Animals

Take a nature walk with your class or an adult family member. List the animals you observe. Draw pictures of foods they might eat and places they could use for shelter.

209

Review and Test Preparation

Vocabulary Review

Use the terms below to complete the sentences. The page numbers tell you where to look if you need help.

nectar p. 180   hibernate p. 194
forage p. 189   prairie p. 200
migrate p. 193   wetland p. 202

1. To move and live in another place is to _____.

2. When animals spend the winter in a deep sleep, they _____.

3. A kind of grassland is a _____.

4. A sugary liquid that comes from a flower is _____.

5. A habitat that is covered by water is called a _____.

6. When animals wander to different places to find food, they _____.

Check Understanding

7. What happens to the leaves of the Ohio Buckeye in fall?

    A. They turn green.

    B. They fall off.

    C. They start to grow again.

    D. They get bigger.

8. Compare these habitats.

How are they alike and different?

Critical Thinking

9. Why do some animals need to change colors when the season changes?

10. Why would it be hard for some animals in a forest to live on a prairie?

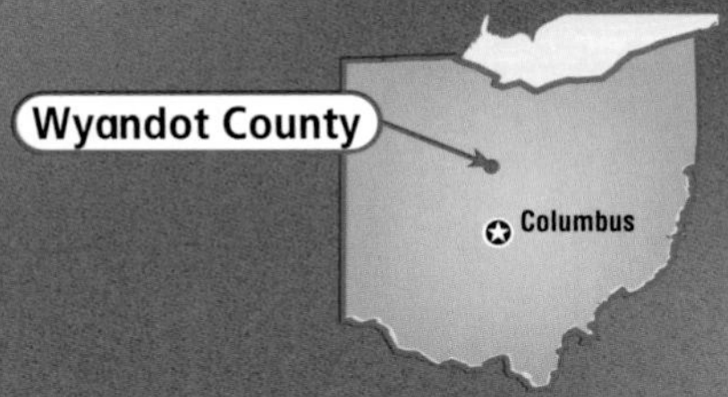

Wyandot County
Columbus

Eagle Nesting Sites

There are more bald eagles in Ohio now than there once were.

In 1979, there were only four pairs of nesting bald eagles in Ohio. The reason is that they lost their habitat in the tall trees near water. The trees help keep them and their young safe. When people cleared the land, they chopped down the trees. The eagles that lived there had to find a new place to nest.

young eagle in its nest

People once destroyed the bald eagles' homes.

Today, there is good news. There are now 107 bald eagle nests in Ohio. People have made laws to protect the eagles. They have even moved young eagles into new nests.

Many of the eagles live near Lake Erie. Some eagles live in trees near other lakes and rivers. Today, there are seven pairs of bald eagles in Wyandot County.

Now people are helping the eagles.

Bald eagles nest near water.

Think and Do

I. **SCIENTIFIC THINKING** Eagles usually use the same nest every year. Draw a picture to show how taking away the trees put the bald eagles in danger.

2. **SCIENTIFIC THINKING** Look in a book or online to find out where else bald eagles live in the United States. Find out more about what people are doing to help these birds. Write sentences to tell how people protect the bald eagle.

LS-1 Explore organisms' basic needs; **LS-2** Identify environments; **LS-3** Explain need for habitats; **LS-5** Explain need for food; **LS-7** Compare Ohio habitats; **LS-8** Compare Ohio animal activities; **ST-1** Explain technology benefits/risks; **ST-2** Investigate how technology meets needs; **ST-3** Predict technology effects; **SI-10** Communicate explanations; **SK-3** Describe the effects of science on people and the environment

213

Columbus

White-Tailed Deer

The white-tailed deer is Ohio's state animal. You have probably seen white-tailed deer. They live in wooded areas in Ohio. But that has not always been the case.

Before 1904, many white-tailed deer lived here. But from 1904 to 1923, there were few deer. Settlers hunted and killed them. There were no laws to protect the deer.

The deer lost their homes when people cut down the forests. So, with fewer places to live and less food, many of the deer died.

The white-tailed deer is Ohio's state animal.

To help the deer, people made laws to control deer hunting. This allowed the deer to survive. People also set up safe places for the deer to raise their young. These places gave the deer shelter, water, and plenty of food. There are now more than 450,000 white-tailed deer in Ohio.

white-tailed deer

Think and Do

1. **SCIENTIFIC THINKING** Pretend you are making a safe place for white-tailed deer to live. What will this place need to help the deer survive? Make a poster advertising your new home for deer.

2. **SCIENCE AND TECHNOLOGY** Scientists use computers to keep track of white-tailed deer and where they live. What kinds of information about deer do you think the scientists keep? Make a list of the important things you would keep track of if you were looking after the deer.

LS-1 Explore organisms' basic needs; **LS-2** Identify environments; **LS-3** Explain need for habitats; **LS-5** Explain need for food; **LS-7** Compare Ohio habitats; **LS-8** Compare Ohio animal activities; **ST-1** Explain technology benefits/risks; **ST-2** Investigate how technology meets needs; **ST-3** Predict technology effects; **SI-10** Communicate explanations; **SK-3** Describe the effects of science on people and the environment

215

Columbus → Columbus

Columbus Zoo

What could you learn by visiting a gorilla that lives in a cage? You could see what it looks like and maybe hear it make sounds. That's about it.

But what if you could visit gorillas in a forest setting? You would see how they share the woods with other animals. You would also see how gorillas live and how they treat one another. This is why the Columbus Zoo and Aquarium provides natural settings for its animals.

The zoo has built communities for endangered animals to live in. This helps us learn how we can save them.

Columbus Zoo

The zoo also has a special program that helps species in danger have more young. One endangered animal is the West Indian manatee. Boats hurt or kill many manatees. The zoo is trying to help them survive.

The zoo built a home for the manatees. There is a large pool of water with islands along a muddy beach. Mangrove trees grow on the shore. Birds and insects fly through the air. Giant doors in the roof open to let in the sunlight, wind, and rain.

West Indian manatees

Think and Do

1. **SCIENCE AND TECHNOLOGY** Suppose you live in a town on the coast of Florida. You are asked to help save manatees. Use words and pictures to describe how you would help save the manatees from being hurt by motorboats. What problems might your solution cause?

2. **SCIENTIFIC THINKING** What does an animal need to stay well and happy in a zoo home? Choose an animal, and draw a picture of a new home you would build at the zoo. Write to describe how this new home would help keep the animal healthy and happy.

Keeping Streams Clean

Materials
- plastic container
- water
- vegetable oil

What to Do

1. Fill the container with water.
2. Add a small amount of oil to the water.
3. What happens? Communicate what you observe.

Draw Conclusions

1. If something oily got into a stream, what might it do to the animals who lived there?
2. If a bald eagle ate a fish or drank some water from this stream, what might happen to the bald eagle?
3. Why is it important to keep water clean?

LS-1 Explore organisms' basic needs; **LS-2** Identify environments; **LS-3** Explain need for habitats; **LS-5** Explain need for food; **LS-7** Compare Ohio habitats; **LS-8** Compare Ohio animal activities; **ST-1** Explain technology benefits/risks; **ST-2** Investigate how technology meets needs; **ST-3** Predict technology effects; **SI-10** Communicate explanations; **SK-3** Describe the effects of science on people and the environment

Habitat Diorama

Materials
- empty shoe box
- scissors
- tape or glue
- old magazines with pictures of animals
- construction paper
- string

What to Do

1. Choose either the bald eagle or the white-tailed deer. Find pictures and cut them out. (Ask before you cut them out.)

2. Now list the things this animal needs to live. For example, eagles need tall trees to make their nests in.

3. Make a diorama of the animal and its environment. Show the things that every animal needs in order to survive—shelter, food, and water. Explain your diorama to your class.

Draw Conclusions

1. How might a list of things that animals need to survive help you protect animals in the wild?

2. How does making a model help you understand what animals need?

LS-1 Explore organisms' basic needs; LS-2 Identify environments; LS-3 Explain need for habitats; LS-5 Explain need for food; LS-7 Compare Ohio habitats; LS-8 Compare Ohio animal activities; SI-10 Communicate explanations

219

Five Rivers
Fountain of Light → • ✪ Columbus

Physical Sciences

The chapter and features in this unit address these Grade Level Indicators from the Ohio Academic Content Standards for Science.

Unit C Ohio Expeditions

The investigations and experiences in this unit also address many of the Grade Level Indicators for standards in Science and Technology, Scientific Inquiry, and Scientific Ways of Knowing.

TO: Gail@hspscience.com
FROM: Silvia@hspscience.com
RE: Five Rivers Fountain of Lights

Dear Gail,

Have you ever seen a laser light show?
I did. It was in Dayton, where five rivers
meet. You've never seen anything like it!
The lasers on the water made everything
glow. Wish you could have been there.

Bye,
Silvia

Experiment!

Drum Sounds In this unit, you will learn about sound. How can you make different sounds on a drum sound? Plan an experiment and find out!

Chapter 6

Sound and Light

Vocabulary

sound
vibrate
sound wave
loudness
pitch
reflect

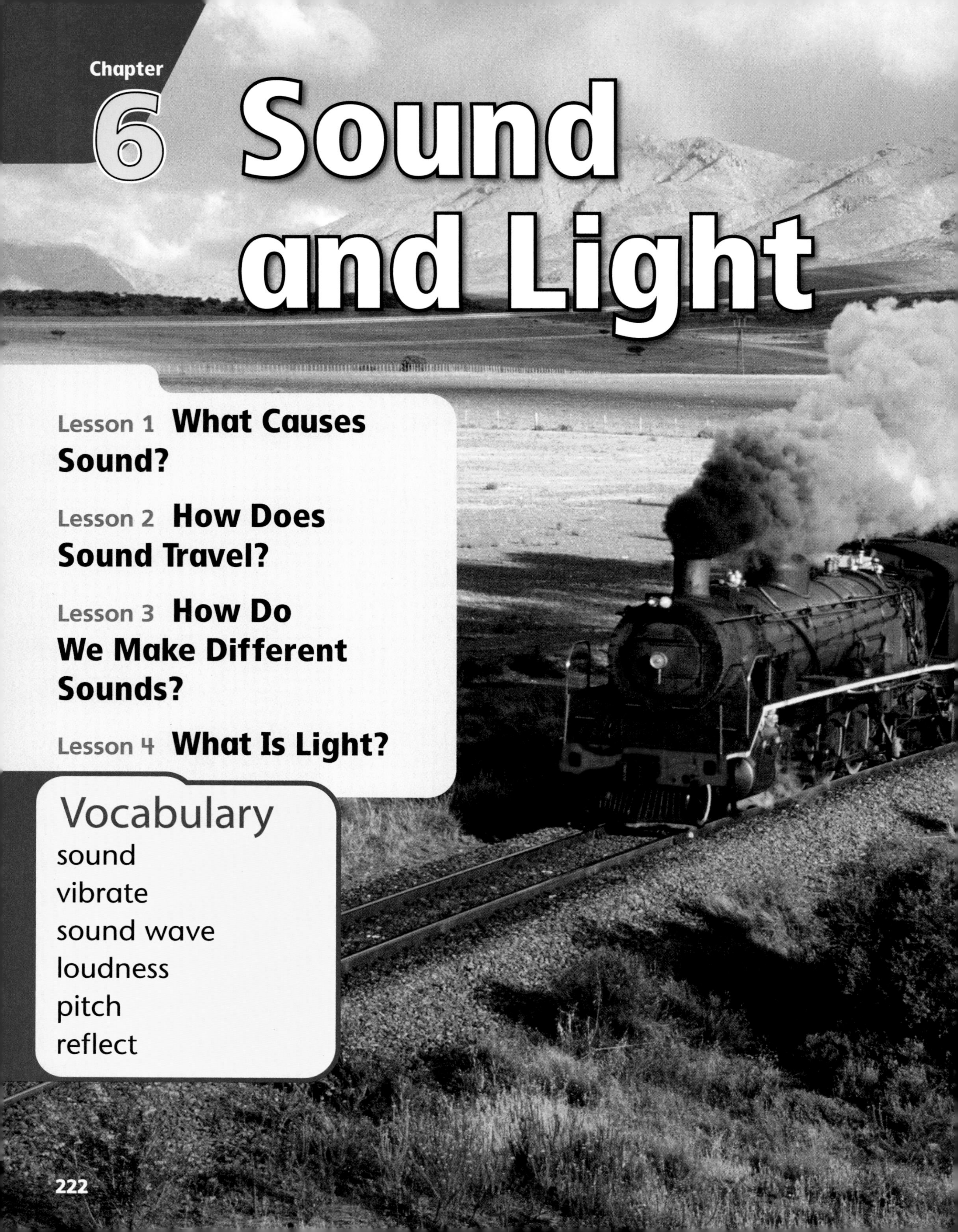

I wonder...

Why can people who are far away from this train hear the sounds it makes?

What do YOU wonder?

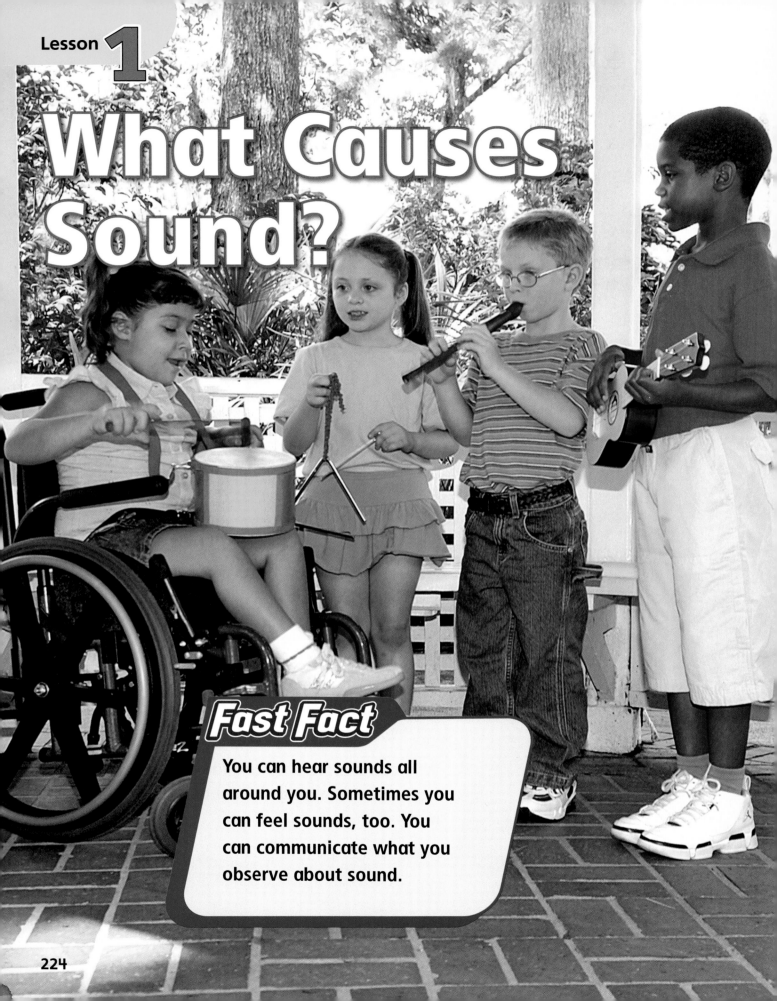

What Causes Sound?

Fast Fact

You can hear sounds all around you. Sometimes you can feel sounds, too. You can communicate what you observe about sound.

How Sound Is Made

You need

 • **wax paper** • **tube with holes** • **rubber band**

Step 1

Put wax paper over one end of a tube. Use a rubber band to hold the wax paper in place.

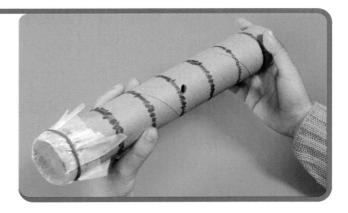

Step 2

Hum into the open end of the tube. What do you hear? Feel the wax paper. What do you feel? Stop humming. What changed?

Step 3

Communicate your observations to a classmate.

Inquiry Skill
When you **communicate**, you share your ideas through writing, drawing, or speaking.

VOCABULARY
sound
vibrate

READING FOCUS SKILL

CAUSE AND EFFECT Look for the causes of sounds.

Vibrations Make Sound

Sound is energy that you can hear. You may hear a dog barking or a bell ringing. You may hear music playing or people talking. The sounds are different, but they are made in the same way. All sound is made when something **vibrates**, or moves quickly back and forth.

What things in these pictures are making sounds?

What things in these pictures are making sounds?

Objects make sounds when they vibrate. The top of a drum vibrates when you hit it. A guitar string vibrates when you pluck it. The vibrations make sounds. When the vibrations stop, the sounds stop. Some things, such as a drum or thunder, make sounds so loud that you can feel them, too.

⭐ **CAUSE AND EFFECT** What causes sound?

Insta-Lab

Make Vibrations

Hold a ruler on a desk so that one end hangs over the edge. Push that end down, and then let it go. What do you see, hear, and feel?

The Ear

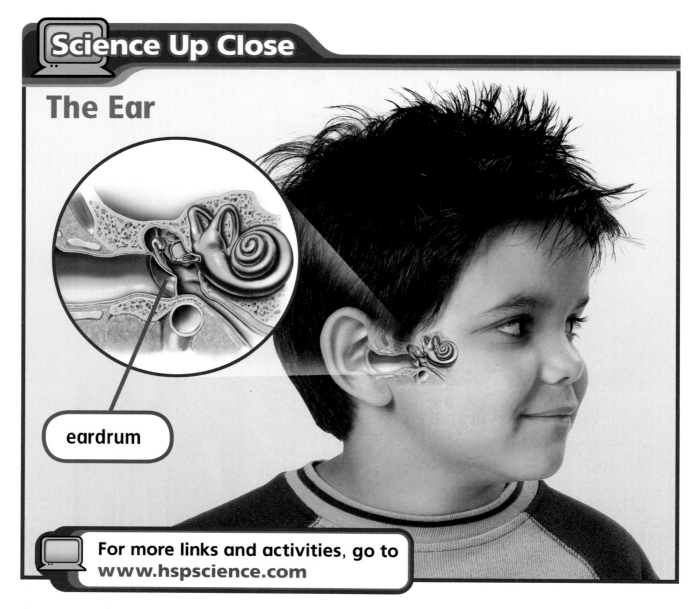

eardrum

For more links and activities, go to
www.hspscience.com

How You Hear

You hear sounds with your ears. Sound
vibrations move through the air into your
ear. They move from your outer ear to your
inner ear. The vibrations cause the eardrum
and the tiny bones in your ear to vibrate.
The inner ear sends signals to the brain.
You hear a sound.

CAUSE AND EFFECT What causes you to hear
a sound?

Focus Skill

1. CAUSE AND EFFECT Copy and complete this chart. Tell the effect of each cause.

cause		effect
Something vibrates.	→	You hear Ⓐ _____ .
Something stops vibrating.	→	The sound Ⓑ _____ .
Vibrations move through the ear.	→	The eardrum Ⓒ _____ .

2. SUMMARIZE Write two sentences that tell what this lesson is about.

3. VOCABULARY Use the terms **vibrate** and **sound** to tell how sound is made.

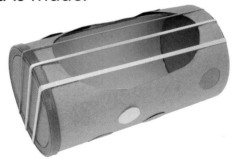

Test Prep

4. What happens when a guitar string stops vibrating?
   A. The sound gets louder.
   B. The sound stops.
   C. The eardrum vibrates.
   D. The sound gets softer.

Links

Writing

Description of Sounds
Sit quietly, and listen to the sounds around you. Then write about the sounds you hear. Describe the way they sound.

I hear a door squeak.

A dog barks outside.

 For more links and activities, go to www.hspscience.com

How Does Sound Travel?

Fast Fact

Most sound you hear travels through the air to reach your ears. Sound can also travel through solids, such as wood, and through liquids, such as water. You can use what you know to predict how a sound will travel.

How Sound Travels

You need

● **tape measure**

● **masking tape**

Step 1

Use the tape measure to measure 50 centimeters on your desk. Mark each end with tape.

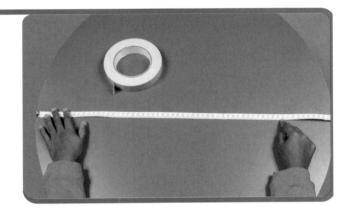

Step 2

Scratch at one tape mark and listen at the other. **Predict** whether you will hear the sound if you put your ear on the desk. Try it.

Step 3

What did you observe? Was your **prediction** correct?

Inquiry Skill

To **predict**, think about what you already know and then tell what you think will happen.

PS-1 Explore sound production; SI-6 Use observations; SI-9 Use numbers

VOCABULARY
sound wave

(Focus Skill) READING FOCUS SKILL

MAIN IDEA AND DETAILS Look for the different kinds of matter that sound can travel through.

Sound Travels Through Air

Sound can travel through different kinds of matter. Sound can travel through gases, such as air. When an object vibrates, it produces sound waves. **Sound waves** are vibrations that are moving through matter. The sound waves travel through the air to your ears, and you hear the sound.

Sound moves in all directions. When a rooster crows, people all around the rooster can hear it.

Sound waves can be blocked. Some people use ear coverings to protect their ears from loud sounds. This keeps some of the sound waves from reaching their eardrums.

⭐ **MAIN IDEA AND DETAILS** **How does sound move?**

233

Sound Travels Through Water

Sound travels through liquids, such as water. Sound travels faster through water than through air.

Dolphins make sounds to find things underwater. The sounds travel through the water. When they hit objects, they bounce off. The bounced sounds are called echoes. The dolphins listen to the echoes to tell how far away things are.

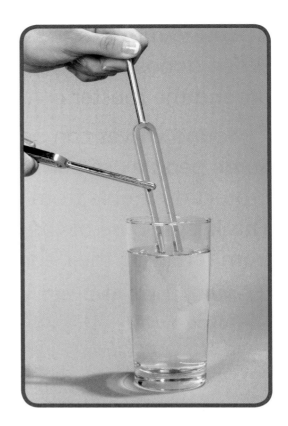

▲ Sound waves from the tuning fork move through the water. They make the water vibrate.

▼ dolphin

▲ humpback whales

Humpback whales also make sounds underwater. Their sounds are like songs. The whales may sing for many hours at a time. Their songs can reach other whales that are far away.

 **MAIN IDEA AND DETAILS** What is one liquid that sound can travel through?

Make Waves

Fill a cup with water. Gently touch the water with a pencil eraser. What do you see? Tell a classmate how the ripples are moving. How are these little waves like sound waves?

Sound Travels Through Solids

Sound travels through solids, such as wood and glass. Sound travels faster through most solids than through gases or liquids.

Have you ever talked on a string telephone? A string connects two cans. One person talks into a can. The sound waves make the air in the can vibrate. This makes the can vibrate, and then the can makes the string vibrate.

The sound waves travel through the string and make the other can and the air in it vibrate. The vibrations travel into that person's ear, and he or she hears the sound.

MAIN IDEA AND DETAILS In a string telephone, how does sound travel from one can to the other?

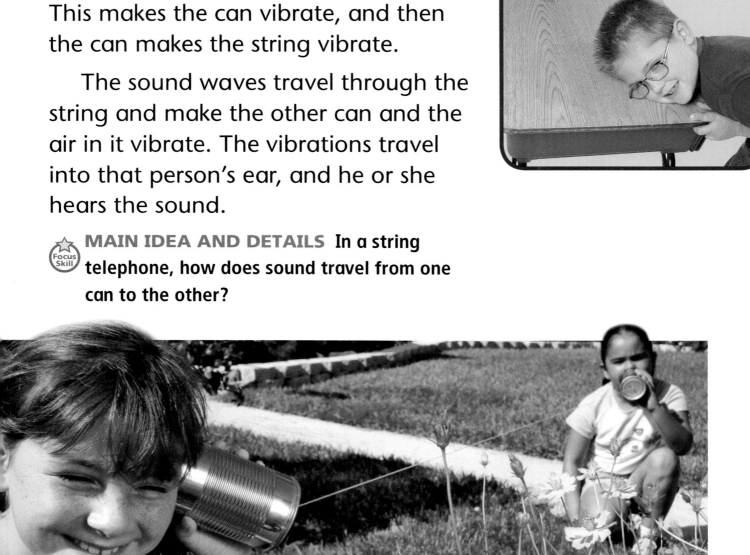

1. MAIN IDEA AND DETAILS Copy and complete the chart. Tell about the kinds of matter that sound can travel through.

Main Idea and Details

Sound travels through different kinds of matter.

| Sound can travel through air, which is a Ⓐ _____. | Dolphins make sounds that travel through water, a Ⓑ _____. | Sound travels through Ⓒ _____, such as wood and glass. |

2. DRAW CONCLUSIONS How can you tell that sound travels in all directions?

3. VOCABULARY Use the term **sound waves** to tell about the picture.

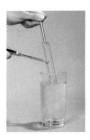

Test Prep

4. Which kind of matter does sound travel through the fastest?
A. solids
B. liquids
C. gases
D. liquids and gases

Links

Math

Order from Least to Most
Sound travels at different speeds through different kinds of matter. Use the chart to order the speeds from slowest to fastest.

Speed of Sound in Meters per Second

kind of matter	speed
water	1,433
glass	5,030
air	343
gold	3,240
rubber	1,600

For more links and activities, go to www.hspscience.com

How Do We Make Different Sounds?

Fast Fact

Guitar strings make different sounds because they are not all the same. Some are thick. Some are thin. Some are tighter than others. You can hypothesize why sounds are different.

Why Sounds Are Different

You need

- colored water
- 3 glasses
- wooden spoon

Step 1

Pour a different amount of water into each glass. **Hypothesize** whether all the glasses will sound the same when you tap them.

Step 2

Use the spoon to tap each glass on the side. Was your **hypothesis** correct?

Step 3

Find a way to make all the glasses sound the same.

Inquiry Skill

When you **hypothesize**, you make an explanation that you can test.

VOCABULARY
loudness
pitch

 READING FOCUS SKILL

CAUSE AND EFFECT Look for what causes different sounds.

Loud or Soft

Sounds are different. They may be loud or soft. A shout is a loud sound. A whisper is a soft, or quiet, sound.

The **loudness** of a sound is how loud or soft it is. It takes more energy to make a loud sound than a soft sound.

The closer you are to what makes a sound, the louder the sound you hear. It's hard to hear people talk when you are far away from them. As you move closer, you can hear them more easily.

CAUSE AND EFFECT What happens when a lot of energy is used to make a sound?

Insta-Lab

Loud and Soft

Clap as loudly as you can. Then clap as softly as you can. Does it take more energy to clap loudly or to clap softly?

Talk Quietly

High or Low

Sounds are also different in **pitch**, or how high or low they are. A whistle makes a sound with a high pitch. A big drum makes a sound with a low pitch.

The speed of an object's vibration makes its sound's pitch low or high. Thicker or longer strings vibrate more slowly. They make a sound with a low pitch. Thinner or shorter strings vibrate faster. They make a sound with a high pitch.

Focus Skill **CAUSE AND EFFECT** What makes a sound's pitch high or low?

A xylophone has long and short bars. The long bars make sounds with low pitches. The short bars make sounds with high pitches. ▼

242

1. CAUSE AND EFFECT Copy and complete this chart. Tell what sound is the effect of each cause.

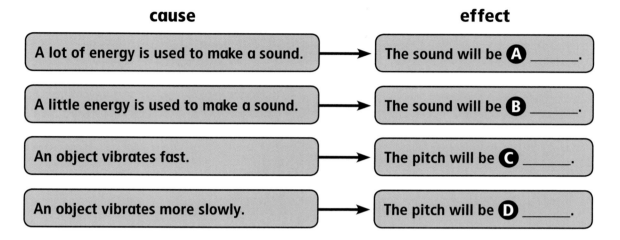

cause	effect
A lot of energy is used to make a sound.	→ The sound will be **Ⓐ** _____.
A little energy is used to make a sound.	→ The sound will be **Ⓑ** _____.
An object vibrates fast.	→ The pitch will be **Ⓒ** _____.
An object vibrates more slowly.	→ The pitch will be **Ⓓ** _____.

2. SUMMARIZE Write a summary of this lesson. Begin with the sentence **Sounds are different**.

3. VOCABULARY Explain the meanings of the terms **loudness** and **pitch**.

Test Prep

4. What happens when a string vibrates very quickly?
  A. It makes a high sound.
  B. It makes a low sound.
  C. It makes no sound.
  D. It makes a soft sound.

Links

Social Studies

Too Many Sounds
Too many sounds can cause noise pollution. Make a list of problems caused by too much sound. Then, for each sound problem, write a way people could solve it.

Noise Pollution

problem	solution
The radio and television are both on.	Turn one off.

For more links and activities, go to www.hspscience.com

What Is Light?

Fast Fact

Light moves in straight lines. When something stops light from moving forward, it makes a shadow. You can draw conclusions about the way light moves.

How Light Moves

You need

- small mirror

- flashlight

Step 1

Choose a spot on the wall on which you want light to shine. Then hold up the mirror.

Step 2

Have a partner shine the flashlight onto the mirror. Move the mirror so that light shines onto the spot you chose.

Step 3

Draw conclusions about the way light moves.

Inquiry Skill

Use your observations and what you know to draw conclusions.

Reading in Science

VOCABULARY
reflect

READING FOCUS SKILL

MAIN IDEA AND DETAILS Look for details about how light moves.

Light

Light is a form of energy that lets you see. Most light seems to have no color, but it can actually be made up of many colors.

You can see the colors in light when you look at a rainbow. A rainbow forms when sunlight passes through drops of water in the air. The water splits the light into all of its colors. What colors do you see in the rainbow?

A glass prism acts like drops of water in the air. It splits the light into all of its colors. ▼

rainbow

Light travels in straight lines. A flashlight shines light toward the spot at which you point it.

When light hits most objects, the objects **reflect**, or bounce, light. You can see objects because they reflect light. Different objects reflect different amounts of light. A white, smooth surface reflects more light than a dark, rough one. Most mirrors are smooth and flat. They reflect most of the light that hits them.

 MAIN IDEA AND DETAILS How does light move?

Shadows

Light can pass through some objects but not others. An object that blocks light makes a shadow. When trees block sunlight, they make shadows on the ground.

Look at the picture of the people in the room. Light can pass through the glass windows. What is blocking the light? How can you tell?

 MAIN IDEA AND DETAILS
What makes a shadow?

Insta-Lab

What Does Light Shine Through?

Shine a flashlight onto different materials. You might try wax paper, plastic wrap, newspaper, and construction paper. Which ones does light pass through? Communicate your results.

1. MAIN IDEA AND DETAILS Copy and complete this chart. Tell details about light.

Main Idea and Details

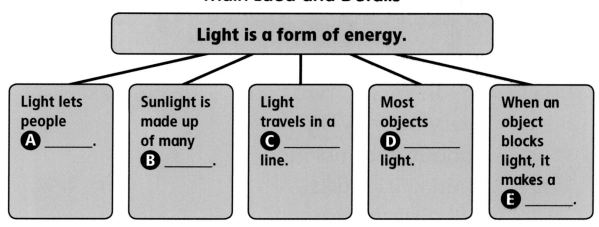

Light is a form of energy.

| Light lets people **A** _____. | Sunlight is made up of many **B** _____. | Light travels in a **C** _____ line. | Most objects **D** _____ light. | When an object blocks light, it makes a **E** _____. |

2. DRAW CONCLUSIONS How can you tell if light can not pass through an object?

3. VOCABULARY Use the term **reflect** to tell about light.

Test Prep

4. Why do only some objects make shadows?

Links

Math

Measure Shadows

Stand a pencil in a piece of clay. Put it in a sunny place. Measure its shadow. Record in a chart the time and the shadow's length. Wait one hour. Measure the shadow again, and record its length. Repeat one hour later.

A Pencil's Shadow

time	length of shadow
9:00	5 inches
10:00	4 inches
11:00	3 inches

 For more links and activities, go to **www.hspscience.com**

249

PS-1 Explore sound production; **ST-2** Investigate how technology meets needs

The Sounds Spring Brings

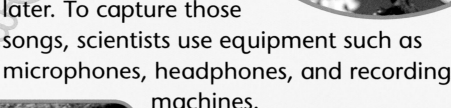

In spring, birds are very busy flying about and making nests. Scientists who study birds often try to record bird songs to study later. To capture those songs, scientists use equipment such as microphones, headphones, and recording machines.

Trickle, Trickle

Spring brings warmer weather. Warm weather melts any snow and ice left from winter. The melted water trickles through streams and rivers and into lakes and oceans.

Whoosh, Whoosh

Spring brings whooshing winds. The wind blows clouds and kites in the sky. Wind also helps plants spread their seeds. When seeds land, they grow into new plants and flowers.

Buzz, Buzz

Spring brings new plants and flowers. Busy bees buzz from flower to flower collecting nectar. Nectar is a sweet liquid made by flowers. The buzzing bees collect nectar for food to eat.

Phonics Fun

Whoosh has the *sh* sound. What are five other words with the same sound?

Think About It

What are some sounds heard in other seasons?

Find out more! Log on to
www.hspscience.com

A Call to Invent

Alexander Graham Bell is well known as the inventor of the telephone. He was interested in working on machines that used sound. He wanted to help his mother, who could not hear.

About 130 years ago, Bell was trying to improve a machine called a telegraph. It was during this work that he made a discovery. Bell found out that he could send speech over a charged wire. This led to the invention of the telephone.

Moving Sound

What to Do

1. Stretch plastic wrap over the open end of the can. Use the rubber band to keep the plastic tight.

2. Put a spoonful of sugar on the plastic.

3. Hold the metal tray near the can, and bang on the tray with the spoon.

4. Observe what happens to the sugar.

Materials

- plastic wrap
- empty metal can
- rubber band
- sugar
- metal tray
- wooden spoon

Draw Conclusions

What happened? Why did this happen?

Shadows

Shine a flashlight on a wall. Tape paper to the wall where the light hits. Set an object between the wall and the light. Draw and label its shadow on the paper. Then move the object close to the light and far from the light. Draw and label its shadow each time. How does the shadow change? Why does it change?

Review and Test Preparation

Vocabulary Review

Use the terms below to complete the sentences. The page numbers tell you where to look if you need help.

sound p. 226   **pitch** p. 242

vibrate p. 226   **reflect** p. 247

1. When guitar strings move back and forth, they _____.

2. Energy that you can hear is _____.

3. Most objects _____, or bounce, light.

4. The highness or lowness of a sound is its _____.

Check Understanding

5. What causes the sound a drum makes?

   A. ears
   B. loudness
   C. pitch
   D. vibrations

6. What can sound move
through?

F. only gases and liquids
G. only gases and solids
H. only liquids and solids
J. gases, liquids, and solids

7. Why do trees make shadows?
A. Light is made up of many colors.
B. Light can not pass through trees.
C. Light can pass through trees.
D. Light comes from the sun.

Critical Thinking

8. Does it take more energy to whisper or to shout? Explain.

9. What would happen to Earth if there were no sunlight?

Cleveland
Columbus

Severance Hall

outside of Severance Hall

The Cleveland Orchestra begins to play. The sound is perfectly beautiful. Why? It is because of Severance Hall's new design.

When Severance Hall opened, many people came to hear the music. Soon they started to complain about the sound. The designers of the hall had to make a change.

They had to decide what shape to make the new hall. They also had to choose the right materials. If the design and the materials are not right, the music can sound muffled, or unclear.

organ pipes

The hall's new stage is made of wood and other materials. It has curved walls. The walls of the stage are filled with sand. The sand helps to bounce more sound into the audience.

Designers also replaced the shell around the stage. This helped send more sound into the seating area. The organ was hard to hear, so it was moved to the stage, too. All these changes made the music sound great!

inside Severance Hall

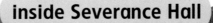

Think and Do

1. SCIENCE AND TECHNOLOGY How did the designers use technology to help make the sound from the orchestra clear and loud? Draw a picture of the stage, and circle the things they changed. How did working together help the designers?

2. SCIENTIFIC THINKING Look carefully at the pictures of Severance Hall. What materials were used to build it? List the materials and tell why you think they were used.

PS-1 Explore sound production; **ST-1** Explain technology benefits/risks; **ST-2** Investigate how technology meets needs; **SI-5** Explain outcomes; **SI-6** Use observations; **SK-3** Describe the effects of science on people and the environment; **SK-4** Explain advantages of teamwork

257

Marblehead Peninsula

Columbus

Marblehead Peninsula Lighthouse

Pretend you are a ship captain sailing around Marblehead Peninsula in Lake Erie. The night is dark, and you can not see. You need help to know where you are and where it is safe to sail. A beam of green light flashes from a lighthouse ahead. You check your chart and see that you should not sail too close to the rocky shore. The light keeps you safe.

The lighthouse was built in 1822. At that time, it used a whale oil lamp. Today, it uses a light that is brighter and stronger.

Marblehead Lighthouse is one of Ohio's oldest lighthouses.

A special lens, called a Fresnel lens, is in a lantern room at the top of the lighthouse. The lens is made of glass circles and looks like a giant beehive. A bulb is inside the lens. As the lens turns around the bulb, it sends out a beam of light.

Thanks to this lens, people can sail safely at night!

The light warns sailors about dangerous areas by blinking its light. Some of the warnings might be "Danger," "Stay Away," "Beware," or "Come This Way."

Think and Do

I. SCIENCE AND TECHNOLOGY Lighthouses use white, green, and red light bulbs to send their signals. Why do you think they use these colors? What do you think each color means? Write down your ideas.

2. SCIENTIFIC THINKING Suppose you were in charge of planning signals used by lighthouses. Make a list of the signals and how they would be shown to the sailors. What colors would you use? How many flashes would each signal have?

PS-3 Explore light; **ST-1** Explain technology benefits/risks; **ST-2** Investigate how technology meets needs; **ST-3** Predict technology effects

259

Wapakoneta

Columbus

Neil Armstrong Air and Space Museum

How would you like to have your hometown name a museum after you? That is what happened to Neil Armstrong, the first person to walk on the moon.

Armstrong and two other astronauts had a lot to learn. They learned how to fly a spacecraft and how to walk on the moon. On July 16, 1969, the astronauts climbed aboard Apollo 11. It took three days to get close to the moon. Then Neil Armstrong and Edwin Aldrin got into the lunar module, called the Eagle.

outside the museum

The astronauts got to where they were supposed to land. But they had a problem. The place was covered with rocks! Armstrong turned off the computer and began to drive the lunar module. The rocket's firing caused dust clouds. This made it hard to see. The module was running out of fuel. Armstrong had to land right away. Slowly and carefully, he lowered the craft onto a clear spot. The <u>Eagle</u> had landed!

Armstrong walks

Think and Do

I. SCIENCE AND TECHNOLOGY Spacecraft have computers that do many things. What are some of the things that a spacecraft's computers do? Why would it be important to have computers to do these things? Write down your ideas.

2. SCIENTIFIC THINKING Write a story about going to the moon. Describe all of the things you had to learn first. Then write about what happened once you got to the moon. Draw pictures to go with your story.

ST-1 Explain technology benefits/risks; **SI-5** Explain outcomes; **SI-6** Use observations; **SK-3** Describe the effects of science on people and the environment

261

Which Materials Absorb Sound?

Materials

- battery radio
- cardboard box that can be closed
- towel
- blanket or pieces of cloth
- newspapers– crumpled or folded
- carpet scraps
- plastic bags
- sweaters
- pillow

What to Do

1. Turn the radio on to play music fairly loudly. Put the radio inside the box and close it. Does the music sound as loud as before?

2. Take the radio from the box. Cover it with the other materials. Which ones absorb sound best?

3. Try the same test with the radio turned to a talk program. Do the same materials work as well as before?

Draw Conclusions

1. Why do you think some materials absorb more sound than others?

2. How might an architect use this information to design a large hall where music is performed?

ST-1 Explain technology benefits/risks; SI-5 Explain outcomes; SI-6 Use observations; SK-3 Describe the effects of science on people and the environment

Lighthouses Around Ohio

Materials
- pictures of Ohio lighthouses
- drawing paper
- crayons or colored pencils
- map of Ohio
- tape or glue

What to Do
1. Compare photographs of lighthouses found in Ohio.
2. Describe each lighthouse on a separate sheet of paper.
3. Attach the photograph to the sheet of paper.

Draw Conclusions
1. How are the lighthouses the same? How are they different?
2. Why do you think some lighthouses are taller than others?
3. How do you think building a lighthouse might affect the environment? How could it prevent bad effects?

References

Contents

Your Senses

You have five senses that tell you about the world. Your five senses are sight, hearing, smell, taste, and touch.

Your Eyes

If you look at your eyes in a mirror, you will see an outer white part, a colored part called the iris, and a dark hole in the middle. This hole is called the pupil.

Caring for Your Eyes

- Have a doctor check your eyes to find out if they are healthy.

- Never look directly at the sun or at very bright lights.

- Wear sunglasses outdoors in bright sunlight and on snow and water.

- Do not touch or rub your eyes.

- Protect your eyes when you play sports.

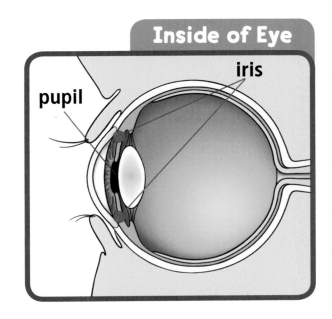

Inside of Eye

pupil, iris

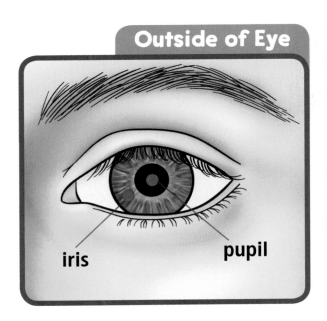

Outside of Eye

iris, pupil

Your Senses

Your Ears

Your ears let you hear the things around you. You can see only a small part of the ear on the outside of your head. The parts of your ear inside your head are the parts that let you hear.

Caring for Your Ears

- Have a doctor check your ears.

- Avoid very loud noises.

- Never put anything in your ears.

- Protect your ears when you play sports.

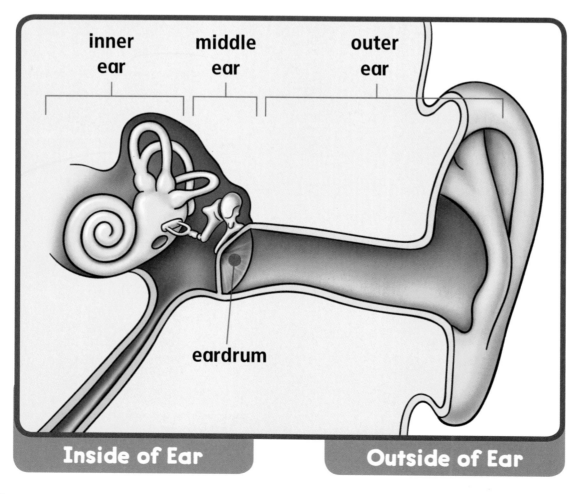

inner ear   middle ear   outer ear

eardrum

Inside of Ear   **Outside of Ear**

Your Senses of Smell and Taste

Your nose cleans the air you breathe and lets you smell things. Your nose and tongue help you taste things you eat and drink.

Your Skin

Your skin protects your body from germs. Your skin also gives you your sense of touch.

Caring for Your Skin

- Always wash your hands after coughing or blowing your nose, touching an animal, playing outside, or using the restroom.

- Protect your skin from sunburn. Wear a hat and clothes to cover your skin outdoors.

- Use sunscreen to protect your skin from the sun.

- Wear proper safety pads and a helmet when you play sports, ride a bike, or skate.

Your Skeletal System

Inside your body are many hard, strong bones. They form your skeletal system. The bones in your body protect parts inside your body.

Your skeletal system works with your muscular system to hold your body up and to give it shape.

Caring for Your Skeletal System

- Always wear a helmet and other safety gear when you skate, ride a bike or a scooter, or play sports.

- Eat foods that help keep your bones strong and hard.

- Exercise to help your bones stay strong and healthy.

- Get plenty of rest to help your bones grow.

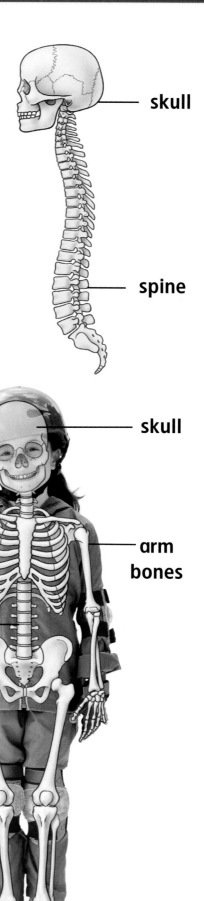

skull

spine

skull

arm bones

spine (backbone)

hip bones

leg bones

Your Muscular System

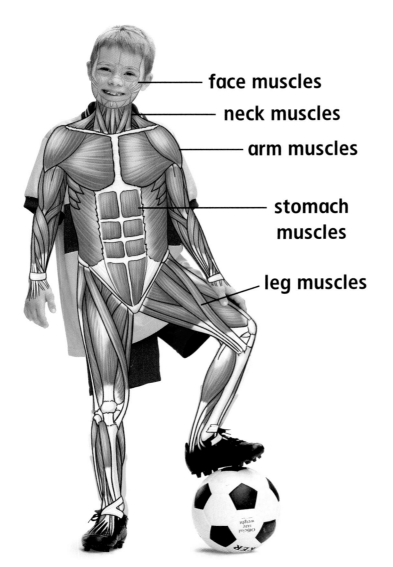

face muscles
neck muscles
arm muscles
stomach muscles
leg muscles

Your muscular system is made up of the muscles in your body. Muscles are body parts that help you move.

Caring for Your Muscular System

• Exercise to keep your muscles strong.

• Eat foods that will help your muscles grow.

• Drink plenty of water when you play sports or exercise.

• Rest your muscles after you exercise or play sports.

Your Nervous System

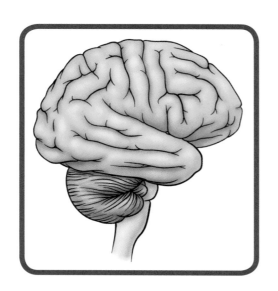

Your brain and your nerves are parts of your nervous system. Your brain keeps your body working. It tells you about the world around you. Your brain also lets you think, remember, and have feelings.

Caring for Your Nervous System

• Get plenty of sleep. Sleeping lets your brain rest.

• Always wear a helmet to protect your head and your brain when you ride a bike or play sports.

Your Digestive System

Your digestive system helps your body get energy from the foods you eat. Your body needs energy to do things.

When your body digests food, it breaks the food down. Your digestive system keeps the things your body needs. It also gets rid of the things your body does not need to keep.

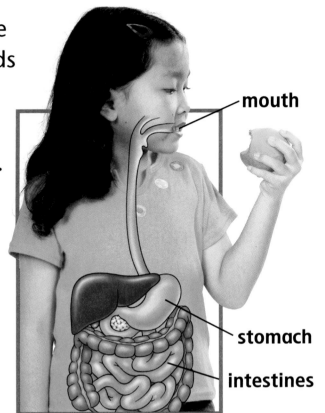

mouth

stomach

intestines

Caring for Your Digestive System

• Brush and floss your teeth every day.

• Wash your hands before you eat.

• Eat slowly and chew your food well before you swallow.

• Eat vegetables and fruits. They help move foods through your digestive system.

Your Respiratory System

You breathe using your respiratory system. Your mouth, nose, and lungs are all parts of your respiratory system.

Caring for Your Respiratory System

- Never put anything in your nose.

- Never smoke.

- Exercise enough to make you breathe harder. Breathing harder makes your lungs stronger.

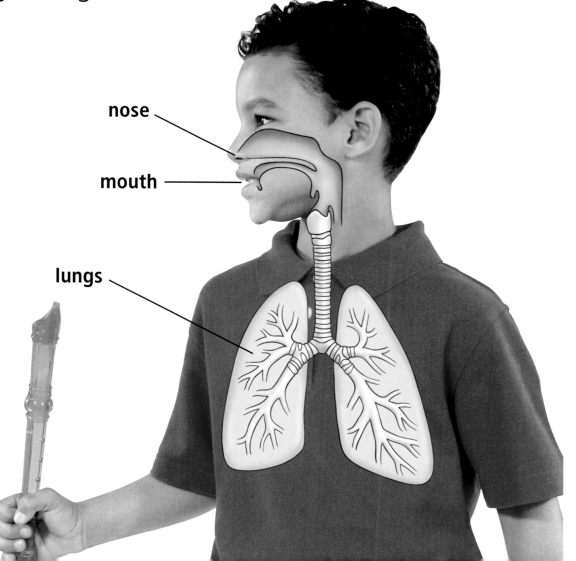

nose

mouth

lungs

Your Circulatory System

Your circulatory system is made up of your heart and your blood vessels. Your blood carries food energy and oxygen to help your body work. Blood vessels are small tubes. They carry blood from your heart to every part of your body.

Your heart is a muscle. It is beating all the time. As your heart beats, it pumps blood through your blood vessels.

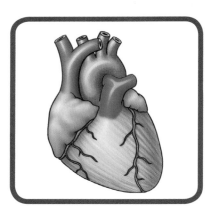

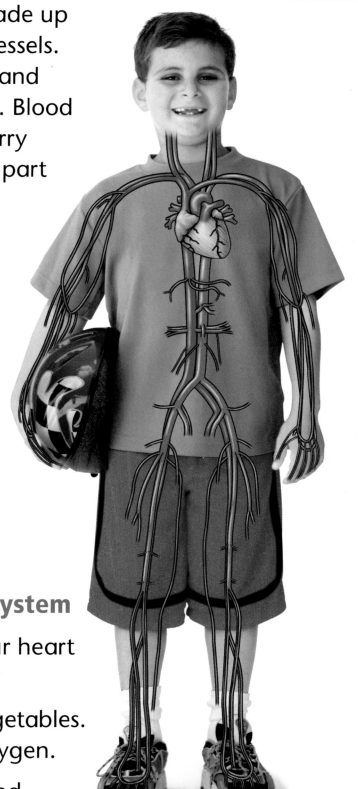

Caring for Your Circulatory System

• Exercise every day to keep your heart strong.

• Eat meats and green leafy vegetables. They help your blood carry oxygen.

• Never touch anyone else's blood.

Staying Healthy

You can do many things to help yourself stay fit and healthy.

You can also avoid doing things that can harm you.

If you know ways to stay safe and healthy and you do these things, you can help yourself have good health.

Getting enough rest

Staying away from alcohol, tobacco, and other drugs

Staying active

Keeping clean

Eating right

Keeping Clean

Keeping clean helps you stay healthy. You can pick up germs from the things you touch. Washing with soap and water helps remove germs from your skin.

Wash your hands for as long as it takes to say your ABCs. Always wash your hands at these times.

- Before and after you eat
- After coughing or blowing your nose
- After using the restroom
- After touching an animal
- After playing outside

Caring for Your Teeth

Brushing your teeth and gums keeps them clean and healthy. You should brush your teeth at least twice a day. Brush in the morning. Brush before you go to bed at night. It is also good to brush your teeth after you eat if you can.

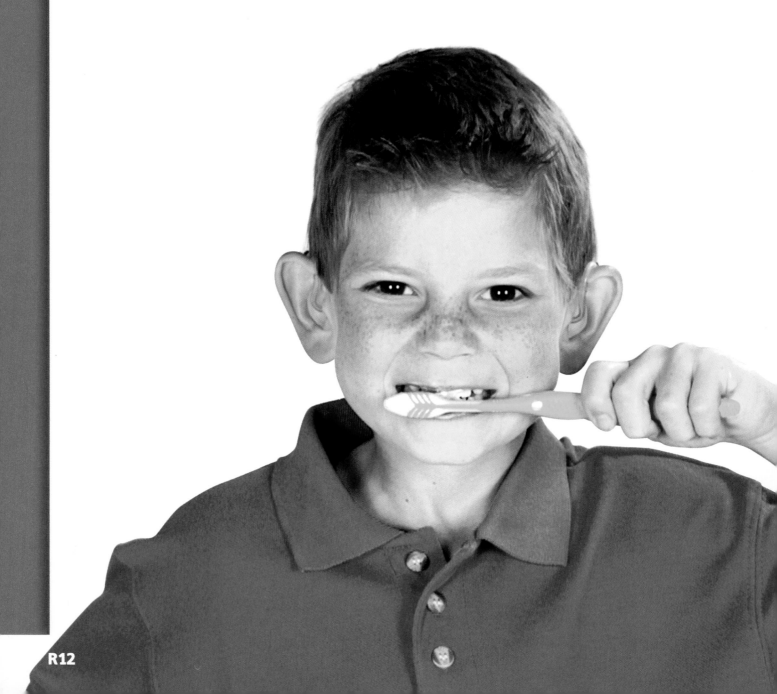

Brushing Your Teeth

Use a soft toothbrush that is the right size for you. Always use your own toothbrush. Use only a small amount of toothpaste. It should be about the size of a pea. Be sure to rinse your mouth with water after you brush your teeth.

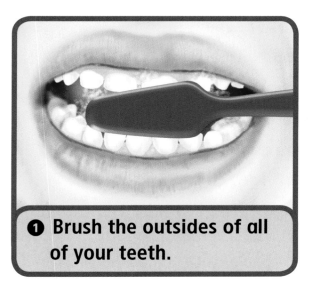

❶ Brush the outsides of all of your teeth.

❷ Brush the insides of all of your teeth.

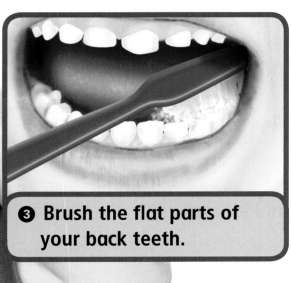

❸ Brush the flat parts of your back teeth.

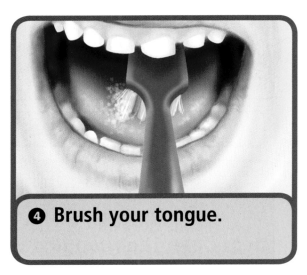

❹ Brush your tongue.

Identify the Main Idea and Details

Learning how to find the main idea can help you understand what you read. The main idea of a paragraph is what it is mostly about. The details tell you more about it. Read this paragraph.

> Snakes swallow their food whole. They cannot chew their food. Snakes' mouths are flexible. They can open their mouths very wide. They can move their jaws from side to side. Their skin can stretch to help open their mouths wide. Because it can open its mouth wide, a snake can swallow a larger animal.

This chart shows the main idea and details.

Detail Snakes cannot chew.	**Detail** Snakes' mouths are flexible.

Main Idea Snakes must swallow their food whole.

Detail Snakes' skin can stretch to help open their mouths wide.	**Detail** Snakes can open their mouths very wide.

Compare and Contrast

(Focus Skill)

Learning how to compare and contrast can help you understand what you read. Comparing is finding what is alike. Contrasting is finding what is different. Read this paragraph.

> The desert and the forest are both environments for living things. Many kinds of plants and animals live there. The desert is dry for most of the year. The forest has more rain. Plants such as cactuses live in the desert. Oak and maple trees live in the forest.

This chart shows comparing and contrasting.

Compare

alike
Both are environments.
Many kinds of plants and animals live in each environment.

Contrast

different
Deserts are dry.
Forests have more rain.
Plants such as cactuses live in the desert.
Oak and maple trees live in the forest.

Cause and Effect

Learning how to find cause and effect can help you understand what you read. A cause is why something happens. An effect is what happens. Some paragraphs have more than one cause or effect. Read this paragraph.

> People once used a poison called DDT to get rid of pests. Small birds eat bugs. Some large birds eat small birds. When small birds ate bugs sprayed with DDT, the DDT got into their bodies. When large birds ate small birds, the DDT got into their bodies, too. DDT caused birds to lay eggs that broke easily.

This chart shows cause and effect.

Cause

Small birds ate bugs sprayed with DDT.

Effects

Large birds that ate small birds got DDT into their bodies. The DDT made the birds lay eggs that broke easily.

Sequence

Learning how to find sequence can help you understand what you read. Sequence is the order in which something happens. Some paragraphs use words that help you understand order. Read this paragraph. Look at the underlined words.

> Ricky and his grandpa made a special dessert. <u>First</u>, Grandpa peeled apples and cut them into small chunks. <u>Next</u>, Ricky put the apple chunks and some raisins in a bowl. <u>Then</u>, Grandpa put the bowl into a microwave oven for about ten minutes. <u>Last</u>, when the bowl was cool enough to touch, Ricky and Grandpa ate their dessert.

This chart shows sequence.

1. <u>First</u>, Grandpa peeled apples and cut them into chunks.

2. <u>Next</u>, Ricky put apple chunks and raisins in a bowl.

3. <u>Then</u>, Grandpa put the bowl in a microwave oven for ten minutes.

4. <u>Last</u>, Ricky and Grandpa ate their dessert.

Draw Conclusions

When you draw conclusions, you tell what you have learned. What you learned also includes your own ideas. Read this paragraph.

> The body coverings of many animals can help them hide. One kind of moth has wings with a pattern that looks like tree bark. The moth is hard to see when it is resting on a tree. A polar bear's white coat can make it hard to see in the snow. Being hard to see can help protect an animal or help it hunt other animals.

This chart shows how to draw conclusions.

What I Read
The body coverings of a moth and a polar bear can help them hide.

What I Know
I have seen an insect that looks like a leaf. The insect was very hard to see when it was on a tree branch.

Conclusion
Some animals that live near my own home have body coverings that help them hide.

Summarize

Focus Skill

When you summarize, you tell the main idea and details you remember from what you read. Read this paragraph.

> The leaves of a tree grow in the summer. They provide food for the growing tree. Leaves trap energy from the sun. They get water from the ground. They take in gases from the air. Leaves use these things to make food for the tree.

This chart shows how to summarize.

Recall Detail Leaves grow in the summer.	**Recall Detail** Leaves trap sunlight.	**Recall Detail** Leaves collect water from the ground and gases from the air.

Summary Leaves use sunlight, water, and gases to make food for the tree.

Using Tables, Charts, and Graphs

Gathering Data

When you investigate in science, you need to collect data.

Suppose you want to find out what kinds of things are in soil. You can sort the things you find into groups.

Things I Found in One Cup of Soil

Parts of Plants

Small Rocks

Parts of Animals

By studying the circles, you can see the different items found in soil. However, you might display the data in a different way. For example, you could use a tally table.

Reading a Tally Table

You can show your data in a tally table.

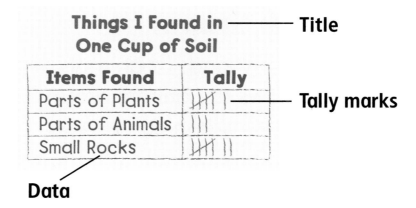

How to Read a Tally Table

How to Read a Tally Table

1. **Read** the tally table. Use the labels.

2. **Study** the data.

3. **Count** the tally marks.

4. **Draw conclusions**. Ask yourself questions like the ones on this page.

Skills Practice

1. How many parts of plants were found in the soil?

2. How many more small rocks were found in the soil than parts of animals?

3. How many parts of plants and parts of animals were found?

Using Tables, Charts, and Graphs

Reading a Bar Graph

People keep many kinds of animals as pets. This bar graph shows the animal groups most pets belong to. A bar graph can be used to compare data.

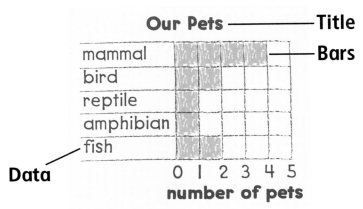

Our Pets ——— Title

Bars

mammal
bird
reptile
amphibian
fish

Data

0 1 2 3 4 5
number of pets

How to Read a Bar Graph

1. **Look** at the title to learn what kind of information is shown.

2. **Read** the graph. Use the labels.

3. **Study** the data. Compare the bars.

4. **Draw conclusions**. Ask yourself questions like the ones on this page.

Skills Practice

1. How many pets are mammals?

2. How many pets are birds?

3. How many more pets are mammals than fish?

Reading a Picture Graph

Some second-grade students were asked to choose their favorite season. They made a picture graph to show the results. A picture graph uses pictures to show information.

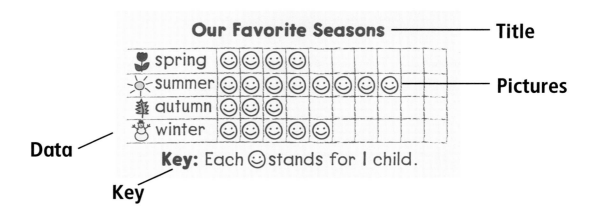

How to Read a Picture Graph

1. **Look** at the title to learn what kind of information is shown.

2. **Read** the graph. Use the labels.

3. **Study** the data. Compare the number of pictures in each row.

4. **Draw conclusions**. Ask yourself questions like the ones on this page.

Skills Practice

1. Which season did the most students choose?

2. Which season did the fewest students choose?

3. How many students in all chose summer or winter?

Measurements

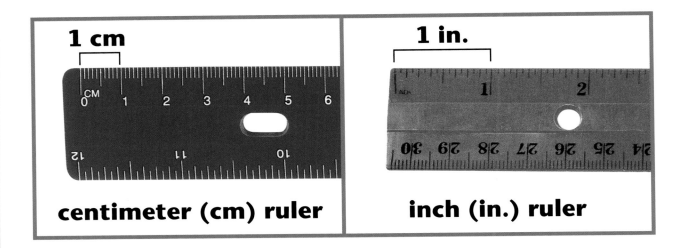

1 cm

centimeter (cm) ruler

1 in.

inch (in.) ruler

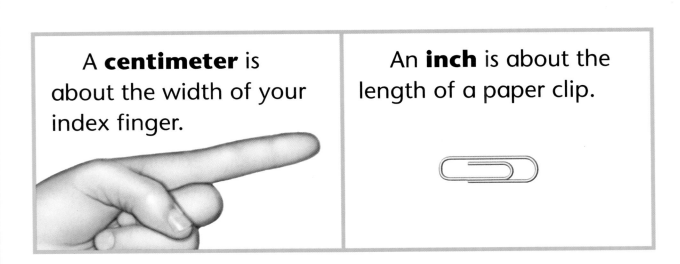

A **centimeter** is about the width of your index finger.

An **inch** is about the length of a paper clip.

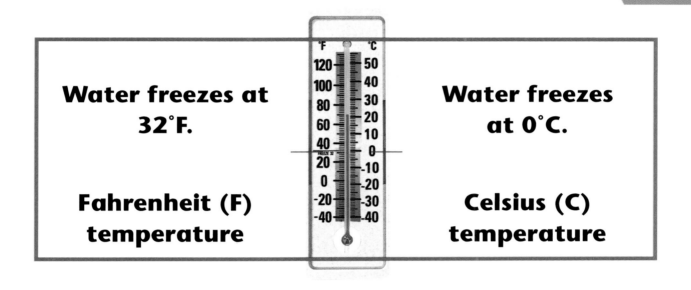

Water freezes at 32°F.

Fahrenheit (F) temperature

Water freezes at 0°C.

Celsius (C) temperature

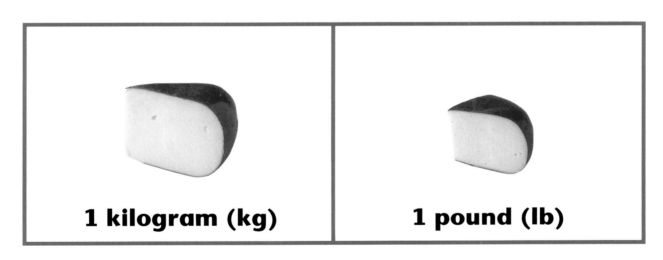

1 kilogram (kg)

1 pound (lb)

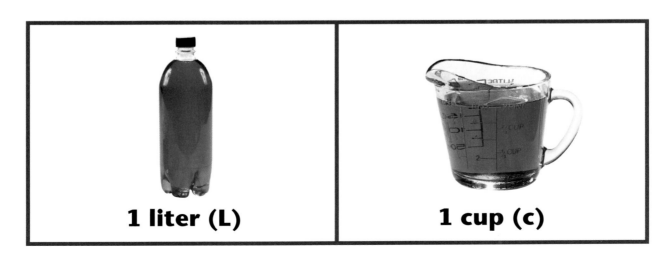

1 liter (L)

1 cup (c)

Safety in Science

Here are some safety rules to follow when you do activities.

1. **Think ahead.** Study the steps and follow them.

2. **Be neat and clean.** Wipe up spills right away.

3. **Watch your eyes.** Wear safety goggles when told to do so.

4. **Be careful with sharp things.**

5. **Do not eat or drink things.**

Visit the Multimedia Science Glossary to see illustrations of these words and to hear them pronounced.
www.hspscience.com

Glossary

A

adapt (uh•DAPT)

To change. Animals and plants adapt over time to live in their environments. (126)

condense (kuhn•DENS)

To change from water vapor gas into liquid water. Water vapor condenses when heat is taken away. (82)

C

camouflage (KAM•uh•flazh)

A way an animal looks that helps it hide. (188)

constellation
(kahn•stuh•LAY•shuhn)

A group of stars that form a pattern. (34)

C

crop (KRAHP)

Plants that people grow and use. (117)

D

desert (DEZ•ert)

An environment that is very dry because it gets little rain. (134)

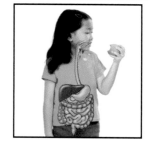

digest (dy•JEST)

To break down food to get energy and nutrients from it. (168)

drought (DROWT)

A long time when it does not rain. During a drought the land may become dry, and plants may die. (84)

E

environment (en•VY•ruhn•muhnt)

All the living and nonliving things in a place. (124)

evaporate (ee•VAP•uh•rayt)

To change from liquid water into a gas. Water evaporates when heat is added. (82)

E

extinct (ek•STINGT)

No longer living. Dinosaurs are extinct because none of them lives anymore. (130)

F

food chain (FOOD CHAYN)

A diagram that shows the order in which animals eat other living things. (158)

food group (FOOD GROOP)

A group of foods that provide many of the same kinds of nutrients. (166)

Food Guide Pyramid

(FOOD GYD PIR•uh•mid)

A chart that helps you choose what foods to eat. The Food Guide Pyramid shows the food groups. (166)

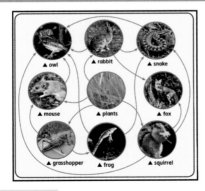

food web (FOOD WEB)

A diagram that shows how food chains are connected. (160)

forage (FAWR•ihj)

To search for food. (189)

F

forest (FAWR•uhst)

A habitat that gets enough rain and warmth for many trees to grow. (198)

G

grassland (GRAS•land)

An open environment covered with grass. (136, 200)

H

habitat (HAB•ih•tat)

A place where a living thing has the food, water, and shelter it needs to live. (125, 198)

hibernate (HY•ber•nayt)

To spend the winter in a deep sleep. (194)

I

inquiry skills
(IN•kwer•ee SKILZ)

A set of skills people use to find out information. (4)

investigate (in•VES•tuh•gayt)

To plan and do a test. Scientists investigate to answer a question. (20)

L

loudness (LOWD•nuhs)

How loud or soft a sound is. (240)

M

migrate (MY•grayt)

To move and live in another place. (193)

moon (MOON)

A huge ball of rock that orbits Earth. The moon takes almost one month to go all the way around Earth. (44)

N

nectar (NEK•ter)

The sugary liquid in flowers. Nectar attracts some butterflies, bees, and birds. (180)

nutrients (NOO•tree•uhnts)

Substances that plants and animals need to survive. Animals get nutrients from food. Plants get nutrients from the soil. (108, 152)

O

ocean (OH•shuhn)

A large body of salt water. Fish, sharks, and other animals live in oceans. (138)

O

orbit (AWR•bit)

The path a planet takes as it moves around the sun. Earth's orbit around the sun takes one year. (33)

oxygen (AHK•suh•juhn)

A gas in the air and water. (108)

P

pitch (PICH)

How high or low a sound is. (242)

planet (PLAN•it)

A large ball of rock or gas that moves around the sun. Earth is our planet. (32)

pond (PAHND)

A small, freshwater environment. Beavers and water lilies may live in a pond. (140)

prairie (PRAIR•ee)

A kind of grassland. Tall grass and wildflowers grow in Ohio prairies. (200)

P

precipitation

(prih•sip•uh•TAY•shuhn)

Water that falls from the sky. Rain, snow, sleet, and hail are kinds of precipitation. (78)

reflect (rih•FLEKT)

To bounce off. Light reflects when it hits most objects. (247)

S

science tools
(SY•uhns TOOLZ)

Tools people use to find information. (12)

R

rain forest

(RAYN FAWR•ist)

An environment, with many tall trees, that gets rain almost every day. (135)

rotate (ROH•tayt)

To spin around like a top. Earth rotates one time every 24 hours. (38)

season (SEE•zuhn)

A time of year that has a certain kind of weather. The four seasons are spring, summer, fall, and winter. (53, 67, 180)

S

shelter (SHEL•ter)

A safe place to live. Birds may use a nest for shelter. (111)

solar system (SOH•ler SIS•tuhm)

The sun, its planets, and other objects that move around the sun. (32)

sound (SOWND)

Energy you can hear. Sounds are made when an object vibrates. (226)

sound wave (SOWND WAYV)

Vibrations moving through matter. When sound waves reach your ears, you can hear sound. (232)

star (STAR)

A big ball of hot gases that give off light and heat energy. The sun is the closest star to Earth. (34)

survive (ser•VYV)

Plants and animals need water to survive. (108)

T

temperature
(TEM•per•uh•cher)

The measure of how hot or cold something is. (75)

thermometer
(ther•MAHM•uh•ter)

A tool that scientists use to measure temperature. (75)

tundra (TUHN•druh)

An environment that is cold and snowy. Plants that live in a tundra are short. The animals have thick fur that helps them stay warm. (137)

V

vibrate (VY•brayt)

To move back and forth quickly. (226)

W

water cycle
(WAW•ter SY•kuhl)

The movement of water from Earth's surface into the air and back to Earth's surface. (82)

weather (WEH•ther)

What the air outside is like. The weather in summer is often sunny and hot. (66)

weather pattern
(WEH•ther PAT•ern)

A change in the weather that repeats. (66)

wetland (WET•land)

A habitat that is covered by water for part of each year. (202)

wind (WIND)

Air that is moving. (76)

Index

Photography Credits

KEY:(t) top, (b) bottom, (l) left, (r) right, (c) center, (bg) background, (fg) foreground

Cover: (front) Joel Satore/National Geographic/Getty Images; (back) (bg) Ken Lucas/Visuals Unlimited; (back) (inset) Mattias Klum/National Geographic/Getty Images;

Front End Sheets: Page 1 Roy Toft/ National Geographic/Getty Images; Page 2 (t) Mattias Klum/National Geographic/Getty Images; (b) Mattias Klum/National Geographic/Getty Images; Page 3 (t) Nigel J. Dennis/Photo Researchers; (b) Wendy Dennis/Visuals Unlimited; (bg for all); Frans Lanting/Minden Pictures;

Title Page: Joel Satore/National Geographic/Getty Images;

Copyright Page: (bg) Ken Lucas/Visuals Unlimited; (inset) Joel Satore/National Geographic/Getty Images;

Back End Sheets: Page 1 (t) Pressnet/Tpoham/The Image Works; (b) Martin Harvey/Peter Arnold, Inc.; Page 2 (t) Martin Harvey/Peter Arnold, Inc.; (b) Mattias Klum/National Geographic/Getty Images; (br) Nigel J. Dennis/Peter Arnold, Inc.; Page 3 (tr) Mattias Klum/National Geographic/Getty Images; (c) Mattias Klum/National Geographic/Getty Images;

Table of Contents
IV-V (b) AP/Wide World Photos; VI-VII (bg) Getty Images.

Unit A
Intro Chapter
26-27 Getty Images; 27 Wayne National Forest, USDA Forest Service.

Chapter 1
28-29 Premium Stock/Corbis; 30-31 Getty Images; 36-37 National Geographic Society/Getty Images; 42-43 Premium Stock/Corbis; 44-45 John Sanford/Science Photo Library/Photo Researchers; 48-49 Amos Nachoum/Corbis; 52-53 Rafael Macia/Photo Researchers; 56-57 NASA; 58 (tr) Corbis, © AP/Wide World Photos; 61 Getty Images.

Chapter 2
62-63 Robert Harding World Imagery/Getty Images; 64-65 Getty Images; 66-67 (bg) Robert Harding World Imagery/Getty Images; 66 (b) PhotoDisc Red (Royalty-free)/Getty Images; 67 (t) Gay Bumgarner/Getty Images; 68 (t) Gay Bumgarner/Getty Images; (c) Mark E. Gibson/Corbis; 69 (b) Getty Images; (t) Gay Bumgarner/Getty Images; 70 (t) Gay Bumgarner/Getty Images; (bl) John Henley/Corbis; (br) Jiang Jin/Superstock; 71 (cl) Gay Bumgarner/Getty Images; 72-73 Joe Raedle/Getty Images; 72 Reuters/NOAA/OSEI/Corbis; 74 (cr) Roland Seitre/Peter Arnold, Inc.; (b) Stephen Mobbs of the Institute for Atmospheric Science, School of the Environment, University of Leeds, UK; 75 (inset) Reuters/NOAA/OSEI/Corbis; 76 Jim Sugar/Corbis; 77 (tr) John Beatty/Photo Researchers; 78 (b) Getty Images; 80-81 Catherine Karnow/Corbis; 84 (inset) Bob Daemmrich/Corbis Sygma; (b) Reuters/Corbis; 85 David Sailors/Corbis; 86 Digital Vision Ltd./SuperStock; 88 (t) Time Davis/Photo Researchers; 89 Johnny Johnson/Animals Animals; 90 Taxi/Getty Images; 91 (bg) Jose Luis Pelaez/Corbis; 93 (tl) Jim Sugar/Corbis; 94 (t) David Parker/Photo Researchers; (b) Mike Dowd/Press-Republican/AP/Wide World Photos; 95 (c) Bob Rowan; Progressive Image/Corbis; 96 (c) Caesar Creek State Park; 97 (t) Richard T. Nowitz/Photo Researchers; 98 (b) Getty Images; 99 (t) Getty Images.

Unit B
Chapter 3
103 (t) Tom Pole/The Holden Arboretum; 104-105 National Geographic/Getty Images; 106-107 Getty Images; 108 (b) Adam Jones/Visuals Unlimited; (cr) David Wrobel/Visuals Unlimited; 109 Inga Spence/Visuals Unlimited; 110 Alamy Images; 111 (t) Kenneth M. Highfill/Photo Researchers; (inset) William Ervin/Visuals Unlimited; 112 Randy Mayor/Getty Images; 113 Photodisc Green (Royalty-free)/Getty Images; 114-115 Getty Images; 116 (t) Karen Bussolini Photography; (b) Kevin R. Morris/Bohemian Nomad Picturemakers/Corbis; (br) David Young-Wolff/PhotoEdit; 117 (bg) Larry Lefever/Grant Heilman Photography; (t) Botanica/Getty Images; 118 Photodisc Green (Royalty-free)/Getty Images; (cr) Barry Runk/Grant Heilman Photography; 118 Getty Images; 119 (t) Michael Boys/Corbis; 120 Tom & Dee Ann McCarthy/Corbis; 122-123 Getty Images; 126 (t) James Watt/Visuals Unlimited; (c) Michael Patrick O'Neill/Photo Researchers, Inc.; 127 images ordered numerically from left to right: (1) Porterfield/Chickering/Photo Researchers, Inc.; (2) Theo Allofs/Visuals Unlimited; (3) Renee Lynn/Corbis; 128 (t) Tierbild Okapia/Photo Researchers; 129 (b) Jacques Jangoux/Photo Researchers; 130 Mark Hamblin/Age Fotostock; Michael Patrick O'Neill/Photo Researchers; 131 (c) James Watt/Visuals Unlimited; 132-133 National Geographic/Getty Images; 134 (t) Digital Vision/Getty Images; (b) Royalty-Free/Corbis; 135 (inset) David M. Schleser/Nature's Images/Photo Researchers, Inc.; (bg) Michael Melford/National Geographic Image Collection; 136 (t) Michel & Christine Denis-Huot/Photo Researchers; (inset) Alamy Images; 137 (t) George D. Lepp/Photo Researchers; (b) Staffan Widstrand/Corbis; 138-139 (t) James Watt/Visuals Unlimited; 139 (c) Jeff Rotman/Photo Researchers, Inc.; (t) James Watt/Visuals Unlimited;140 (t) Superstock; (b) Jane Grushow/Grant Heilman Photography; (inset) Dennis Drenner/Visuals Unlimited; 142 James D Watt/Seapics; 143 (t) Joseph Sohm/Corbis; (cr) Marybeth Angelo/Photo Researchers; 144 National Geographic Images; 145 (bg) Layne Kennedy/Corbis; 147 (cl) Adam Jones/Visuals Unlimited; (cr) David Wrobel/Visuals Unlimited; (bl) Dan Guravich/Corbis; (br) Fletcher and Baylis/Photo Researchers.

Chapter 4
148-149 Getty Images; 150-151 Dan Guravich/Corbis; 152-153 (b) George Grall/National Geographic Image Collection; 152 (t) Royalty-Free/Corbis; 153 (br) Getty Images; 154 (tr) Bill Beatty/Visuals Unlimited; (br) Kevin Schafer/Corbis; (bl) Getty Images; 155 (c) Getty Images; 156-157 Getty Images; 160 (tl) Craig K. Lorenz/Photo Researchers, Inc.; (tc) Arthur C. Smith, III/Grant Heilman Photography; (tr) Getty Images; (cl) Gary Meszaros/Photo Researchers, Inc.; (center-center) David Aubrey/Corbis; (cr) Getty Images; (bl) Gary Meszaros/Visuals Unlimited (bc) Stephen Dalton/Photo Researchers; (br) Adam Jones/Photo Researchers, Inc; 162-163 Jeff Greenberg/Visuals Unlimited; 164 Anthony Nex/Corbis; 165 (tl) Indiana Department of Natural Resources; (bl) Getty Images; (tr) Photodisc Blue (Royalty-Free)/Getty Images; (br) Judith Kramer/The Image Works; 170 AP/Wide World Photos; 172 AP Wide World Photos; 173 (bg) Marcos G. Meider/Age Fotostock America.

Chapter 5
176-177 Mark & Sue Werner/The Image Finders; 178-179 John Lemker/Animals Animals/Earth Scenes; 180 (both) Jim Baron/The Image Finders; 181 (t) Gary Randall/Unicorn Stock Photos; (b) Jim Baron/Baron Photography & Image Finders; 182 (t) Louie Bunde/Unicorn Stock Photos; (c) Gardenphotos.com/Animals Animals/Earth Scenes; (b) Dwight R. Kuhn; 183 Gunter Marx Photography/Corbis; 184 (t) Bob Coury Images/Unicorn Stock Photos; (b) Bruce Coleman, Inc.; 185 (b) Dwight R. Kuhn; 186-187 Hugh Clark; Frank Lane Picture Agency/Corbis; 188 (t) John Conrad/Corbis; (b) Tom Brakefield/Corbis; 189 (t) Tom and Pat Leeson; (cr) Laura Riley/Bruce Coleman; 190-191 (bg) Richard Cummins/Superstock; 190 (tl) Breck P. Kent/Animals Animals/Earth Scenes; (top-center) John M. Burnley/Photo Researchers; (tr) John M. Burnley/Photo Researchers; (b) Jeff Lepore/Photo Researchers, Inc.; 191 (tl) Runk/Schoenberger/Grant Heilman Photography; (tr) Joe McDonald/Animals Animals/Earth Scenes; 192 (t) Erwin & Peggy Bauer/Bruce Coleman; (b) Lynda Richardson/Corbis; 193 (t) Roy Morsch/Corbis; (b) James Urbach/SuperStock; 194 Jeff Lepore/Photo Researchers, Inc.; 196-197 Jeff Greenberg/Alamy; 198-199 (bg) William Manning/Corbis; 198 (t) Sam Fried/Photo Researchers, Inc.; 199 (b) Chris Collins/Corbis; 200 (t) John Lemker/Earth Scenes; (c) Mark & Sue Werner/The Image Finders; (b) Jim Baron/The Image Finders; 201 (b) George D. Lepp/Corbis; (c) Wild & Natural/Animals Animals/Earth Scenes; (b) Ohio Department of Natural Resources; 202 (t) Bruce Coleman, Inc.; (b) AP/Wide World Photos; 203 (t) Gary Meszaros/Photo Researchers, Inc.; (b) Paul M. Butler/The Image Finders; 204 (t) Mike Williams/Ohio Dept. of Natural Resources; (c) Dennis MacDonald/Age Fotostock; (b) David Muench/Corbis; 206 Corbis; 207 Randy Mury/Corbis; 208 (t) IFA/PictureQuest; (c) Courtesy Deb Kessler; (i) Tony Freeman/Photo Edit; 209 (bg) Photodisc Green (Royalty-free)/Getty Images; 211 (c) AP/Wide World Photos; (cr) John Conrad/Corbis; (bl) John Conrad/Corbis; (bc) Tom Brakefield/Corbis; 212 (tr) Bruce Coleman, Inc.; (b) Jim Argo/Unicorn Stock Photos; 213 (tr) Bruce Coleman, Inc.; (cl) Tom Thomson/Spectrum Stock; 214 (b) Bruce Coleman, Inc.; 215 (c) Animals Animals/Earth Scenes; 216 (b) M. Pogany/Columbus Zoo and Aquarium; 217 (c) Lenny Ignelzi/AP/Wide World Photos.

Unit C
Chapter 6
221 (c) Andy Snow © 2003; 222-223 Frans Lemmens/The Image Bank/Getty Images; 226 (bl) Thinkstock (Royalty-free)/Getty Images; (tr) Alamy Images; 227 (t) Alamy Images; (cr) Getty Images; 230-231 Getty Images; 233 (br) E.A. Janes/Age Fotostock America; 234 (b) (ZF) S. Frink/Masterfile; 235 Alamy Images; 240 Getty Images; 244-245 photolibrary.com pty.ltd./Index Stock Imagery; 246 (b) Getty Images; 248 (t) photolibrary.com pty.ltd/Index Stock Imagery; (b) Royalty-free/Corbis; 250 (cr) Steve & Dave Maslowski/Photo Researchers; (bl) Steve Terrill/Corbis; 251 (courtesy) E.R. Degginger/Photo Researchers; 252 (both) Bettmann/Corbis; 255 Photolibrary.com pty. ltd/Index Stock Imagery; 256-257 (all) Roger Mastroianni; 258 (b) Mike Williams: ODNR; 259 (c) Mark Turner/Age Fotostock; 260 (b) Neil Armstrong Air and Space Museum/Ohio Historical Society; 261 (t) NASA.

Glossary:
R27 (tr) Roy Morsch/Corbis; R28 (tl) Larry Lefever/Grant Heilman Photography; (tr) Royalty-Free/Corbis; (cr) Reuters/Corbis; R29 (bl) Images in (bl) frame are numbered clockwise, starting with upper-left image: (1) Craig K. Lorenz/Photo Researchers, Inc.; (2) Arthur C. Smith, III/Grant Heilman Photography; (3) Getty Images; (4) Gary Meszaros/Photo Researchers, Inc.; (5) David Aubrey/Corbis; (6) Getty Images; (7) Gary Meszaros/Visuals Unlimited (8) Stephen Dalton/Photo Researchers; (9) Adam Jones/Photo Researchers, Inc.; R29 (br) Tom and Pat Leeson; R30 (tl) William Manning/Corbis; (cr) Michel & Christine Denis-Huot/Photo Researchers; (cl) National Geographic/Getty Images; (cr) Jeff Lepore/Photo Researchers, Inc.; R31 (tr) James Urbach/SuperStock; (c) George D. Lepp/Corbis; (bl) Getty Images; R32 (bl) Jane Grushow/Grant Heilman Photography; (br) Jim Baron/The Image Finders; R33 (tl) Getty Images; (tr) Michael Melford/National Geographic Image Collection; (br) Rafael Macia/Photo Researchers, Inc.; R34 (tl) National Geographic Society; (cr) E.A. Janes/Age Fotostock America; (bl) Getty Images; (br) Getty Images; R35 (cl) Staffan Widstrand/Corbis; R36 (tr) AP/Wide World Photos; (cl) John Beatty/Photo Researchers, Inc.

FAMILY Meerkats are very social animals.

DESCRIPTION Meerkats are about 12 inches tall when they are standing.

Meerkats have sharp, curved claws.

HABITAT Meerkats build burrows, where they stay at night.